CW00903705

Great Lives, Vital Lessons

A Character Education Curriculum Resource for Grades 5–8

EDITORS

Karen E. Bohlin and Bernice Lerner

CONTRIBUTING AUTHORS

Kathleen Clifford • Deborah Farmer
Kurt Kurtzhals • Alison Reichert
Megan Black Uy • Mary Worlton

Great Lives, Vital Lessons: A Character Education Curriculum Resource for Grades 5–8

Publisher:
Character Development Group, Inc.
P.O. Box 9211
Chapel Hill, NC 27515-9211
919.967.2110, Fax: 919.967.2139
E-mail:
Info@CharacterEducation.com
www.CharacterEducation.com

Copyright © 2005 by The Center for the Advancement of Ethics and Character at Boston University

All rights reserved. No part of this publication may be reproduced or transmitted in any form or by any means, electronic or mechanical, including photography, recording or any information storage and retrieval system, without permission in writing from the publisher.

Martin Luther King Jr.'s "Letter from a Birmingham City Jail" is reprinted on pages 121–128 by arrangement with the Estate of Martin Luther King Jr., c/o Writers House as agent for the proprietor New York, NY. Copyright 1963 Martin Luther King Jr., copyright renewed 1991 Coretta Scott King.

Text editing by Ginny Turner
Layout by Sara Sanders, SHS Design

Library of Congress Control Number: 2004117822
ISBN: 1-892056-41-0
$19.95

Printed in the United States of America

EDITORIAL AND RESEARCH ASSISTANTS
Allison Dalton
Annemarie Haselgrove
Megan Black Uy

DEDICATION
Kevin Ryan

SPECIAL ACKNOWLEDGMENT
Noel Moore

Pueblo 60 School District, Pueblo, CO
through a grant from the
U.S. Department of Education

ACKNOWLEDGMENTS
Susan Dougherty

Paul Gagnon

Thomas Lickona

Molly Marsh

Melissa Moschella

Patricia O'Donovan

Kevin Ryan

Steven S. Tigner

Moira Walsh

WELCOME!

Thank you for taking the time to review the following lessons; we hope you will find them useful and engaging.

These lessons can be integrated into social studies, language arts, or science units as a way of incorporating character education into the existing curriculum. These lessons are not sufficient treatments of each historical figure or of the highlighted virtue; they are designed to ignite the moral imagination of middle school students. Each lesson includes a short biographical profile and useful introductory material. At the end of each lesson we have supplied a bibliography of additional reading, as well as films, websites, and other resources for teachers and students. Many of these sources were used as resources for the biographical information provided within the lessons.

Although these lessons are written for middle school students, teachers may easily adapt any lesson to suit the grade level they teach.[1] Likewise, there is no rigid formula for teaching these lessons. We encourage teachers to use their ingenuity to raise awareness, inspire understanding, promote action, and foster reflection in ways that will help students to deepen their appreciation for biography, as well as the virtues that animate the lives they are studying.

This guide is not intended to substitute for the rigorous and varied ways one can approach the teaching of biography. It is intended to provide supplemental lessons and points of entry for exploring the virtues that help to make each life "great."

It is our hope that you will explore with your students themes of choice and moral courage. By capturing their imaginations and inviting them to experience vicariously the challenges of great lives in history, we hope you can prompt reflection and a heightened commitment to moral action in your students' lives.

---

[1]We have designed these lessons to meet the grade level objectives for the *Massachusetts History and Social Science Framework*. There is, however, enormous overlap among the various state curriculum frameworks. In general, all of the lessons prompt students to "recognize the importance of individual choices, actions, and character" as indicated in the history learning standards for grades 5-8 (79).

Contents

Aristotle's Mean

ARISTOTLE NOTED THE FOLLOWING:

> "Virtue...is a state of character concerned with choice, lying in a mean...it is a mean between two vices, that which depends on excess and that which depends on defect; and again it is a mean because the vices respectively fall short of or exceed what is right in both passions and actions, while virtue both finds and chooses that which is intermediate."
>
> *Nicomachean Ethics*, Book II.6[1]

At the beginning of each lesson a virtue is defined. Where applicable, the moral virtues are graphically illustrated on an Aristotelian scale, with their vice of deficiency to the left and their vice of excess to the right. The definitions provided utilize grade-appropriate language and are referenced throughout the lessons. The Aristotelian scale is intended to show the complexity of virtue and the range of emotions and actions within which a virtuous disposition falls. For example, if courage means knowing what is to be feared and not to be feared, the excess of courage is too little fear and too much bravado, or recklessness. The person who purposely runs out into traffic lacks the appropriate fear of danger, and is displaying a vice rather than a virtue.

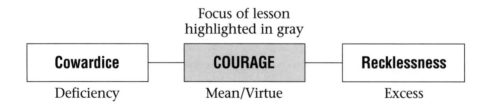

Focus of lesson
highlighted in gray

Cowardice	COURAGE	Recklessness
Deficiency	Mean/Virtue	Excess

---

[1]Aristotle. *Nicomachean Ethics*. Trans. David Ross. New York: Oxford University Press, 1925. p. 39.

The Internalizing Virtue Framework

The Internalizing Virtue Framework is an instructional and schoolwide framework that can help educators be more thoughtful in their efforts to educate for character. Built on the belief that character formation is a lifelong enterprise, the Internalizing Virtue Framework illustrates how we can help students move from an awareness of virtue and good character to the internalization of those habits that constitute good character. The framework is depicted by the triangle with the virtuous life at the apex. In the process of internalizing virtue, awareness, understanding, action, and reflection all play a part.

The Virtuous Life

**Reflection
Action
Understanding**

Awareness

1. *Awareness* of virtue is raised as educators and others explain and define virtues as a means of building a common language and shared character goals for the school community. Students become aware that respect, kindness, and diligence, for example, matter when teachers use these words and remind students of the importance of these virtues to both their intellectual and personal development.

2. *Understanding* of virtue is achieved when students experience that "Aha!" moment; that is, when they realize that living virtuously and making wise choices contributes to personal happiness and the happiness of others. Virtues become less abstract when illustrated by examples. Therefore, understanding is facilitated by stories, poetry, images, music, film, and examples of lives past and present. Understanding heightens students' desire to lead a virtuous life; to use their time, talent, and energy well; and to make wise choices.

3. *Action* enables students to build good habits. We learn by doing. As Aristotle noted, "[Men] become builders by building and lyre-players by playing the lyre;

so too we become just by doing just acts...brave by doing brave acts."[1] Action is about *putting virtue into practice*.

4. *Reflection* involves challenging students to think about what they have done, and to thoughtfully examine the actions of others. Reflection helps students to consider the challenges faced in striving to live virtuously. Did X make a good or a bad decision? Did I make a good or bad decision? Why? What will I do differently next time? Reflection helps students to develop the self-knowledge essential to internalizing virtue. It *cultivates moral reasoning*.

Virtues, once again, are those good habits of mind and character that *dispose individuals to choose and act well*. Fostering virtue is at the heart of character education.

Internalizing virtue is not just about acquiring a set of habits. It is about gradually gaining wisdom—acting and then reflecting on choices and actions, learning from our mistakes, and coming to a greater understanding of how to live a worthwhile life. This continuous cycle is represented by the circle inside the triangle.

---

[1]*Nicomachean Ethics*, trans. David Ross, Oxford: Oxford University Press, 1980, p. 29. II.1.1103a34-7.

WISDOM

WISDOM: The power to judge rightly and follow the best course of action based on knowledge, experience, and understanding.

> **WISDOM***

I have gone without food and sleep in order to think; to no avail: it is better to learn.

—Confucius

*Wisdom is a virtue that does not conform to the doctrine of the mean, because there is no one action or emotion that wisdom moderates. Although a person will not thrive with too little wisdom, one can never have enough. All people who try to acquire the virtue of wisdom must never stop looking to learn and grow, as they will never reach a point when they have all the wisdom they are able to achieve.

This lesson is meant to supplement other lessons on ancient China. Students should have a basic understanding of Confucius's place in history and his reputation as a philosopher. This lesson is intended to introduce students to the virtue of wisdom by referencing Confucius's study and analects. Teachers may want to introduce students to some main points of Confucius's philosophy before beginning the lesson. (See the reference section at the end of this lesson for helpful resources.)

BACKGROUND

The following biographical information is meant to serve as a short description of the life of Confucius. It is suggested that students read a biography such as *Confucius: The Golden Rule* by Russell Freedman before beginning this lesson.

Confucius lived between 551 and 479 B.C.E. During his life he became a local administrator, a minister of justice, a philosopher, and a renowned teacher. His writings and teachings emphasized the importance of humanity and the virtues.

Confucius was born into an age of political turmoil in ancient China. Over the course of his life he was saddened to observe the corruption that was growing rampant in the governmental bureaucracy. Through his study of history, philosophy, and current politics, Confucius formulated his own theories on what constitutes right government. As a philosopher, he delved into antiquity to study lasting truths. He believed that rulers needed to be more like their virtuous ancestors, who had made China strong and enduring. The reason China had survived so long, he suggested, was that the ruler's right to govern came from their own right action. The virtuous emperors of the past had fulfilled their duties to righteousness. To prevent corruption and keep China strong, Confucius taught that rulers must lead by example and cultivate their own virtue.

Confucius traveled through China in search of a position in government in which he could see his theories of government put into action. Although during his lifetime he never held a position higher than a local administrator, a collection of his sayings, *The Analects of Confucius*, became one of the texts most important to Chinese students, and his philosophies and teaching formed the basis for Chinese governmental authority up to the nineteenth century.

His philosophy also placed a strong emphasis on learning. Confucius distinguished learning from thinking. He believed that learning from and contemplating the past was more reasonable and genuine than advancing one's own new ideas. The main tenet of Confucianism, which informs almost all Chinese education, is the belief in the perfectibility of humans through learning. Confucius gained wisdom by analyzing and reflecting on principles from the past and relating them to the present. He considered past truths and contributed his own interpretations to produce timeless insights. Students will learn later that many of his maxims are still relevant to life today.

Awareness | Ask students to define *wisdom*. Record students' answers on the board, then discuss the definition at the beginning of this lesson. Why is wisdom considered a virtue?

Understanding | Teach students about the life of Confucius, then hold a class discussion on wisdom. Ask the following questions (refer to the given definition of wisdom to facilitate answers):

- **How can we gain wisdom?**
- **Where do we get the knowledge, experience, and understanding to judge well?**
- **How can we gain wisdom from Confucius? (Hint: How did Confucius gain wisdom?)**
- **Does learning alone lead to wisdom?**

Ask students to reflect on the following questions. Then ask volunteers to share their thoughts.

- **What wisdom do you need to do well in school? Where would you find the necessary knowledge? Experience?**
- **What wisdom do you need to resist illegal drugs? Where would you find the necessary knowledge?**
- **Do you always need first-hand experience to have wisdom? (No, it is possible to learn from the experiences of others.)**
- **With regard to decision-making, what wisdom have you already gained in your life? How did you gain it? (Through knowledge, experience, example of others, or understanding?)**

Action

Confucius's maxims

Present the following maxims to the students. Discuss what Confucius means to say, and how each maxim is relevant to life today (just as Confucius did with the ancient knowledge he studied). What wisdom can be gained from each? Ask students to rewrite each maxim in contemporary language.

- **To see what is right and not do it, that is cowardice.**
- **The superior men are sparing in their words and profuse in their deeds.**
- **A workman who wants to work well must first prepare his tools.**
- **Not to react after committing an error is in itself an error.**

Invite students to develop and write their own maxims based on their understanding of Confucius' teachings. Post these maxims around the room.

Steps to making decisions

Ask students to create a poster, write a short story, create a flow chart, or draw a cartoon that would help younger students learn how to make wise decisions.

Reflection

An essay on wisdom

Ask students to compose their thoughts on wisdom into an essay(s) using one of the following topic suggestions:

- **Does a person who uses illegal drugs have wisdom? Why or why not? (Use the definition from the beginning of this lesson as a basis for your argument.)**

- **Why is wisdom a virtue? What is the difference between being knowledgeable (smart) and being wise? (Students should recognize that being knowledgeable about facts does not necessarily indicate the ability to make sound decisions.) What is it that leads to wisdom?**

- **When in your life did you practice the virtue of wisdom? Give examples of how you demonstrated wisdom in a particular situation.**

Bibliography

For students and teachers

Confucius image from:
http://search.biography.com/print_record.pl?id=4607

Confucius http://search.biography.com/print_record.pl?id=4607
The Analects of Confucius. Trans. A. Waley. New York: Vintage, 1989.

In questions of science, the authority of a thousand is not worth the humble reasoning of a single individual.

—Quoted in Arago, *Eulogy of Galileo*

DILIGENCE

DILIGENCE: The habit of making a constant and earnest effort to accomplish what is undertaken; persistence; active engagement; industriousness.

Deficiency: Laziness	DILIGENCE	Excess: Workaholism

This lesson is intended to be taught in conjunction with a science or mathematics class when studying the contributions of Galileo. His life may be introduced when discussing scientists, scientific method, the solar system, properties of matter, physics, etc. The lesson is designed to highlight Galileo's diligence and to prompt students to think about diligence in their daily lives. Ideally, students will be familiar with the Renaissance before this lesson is taught.

BACKGROUND

The following biography provides a brief overview of Galileo's accomplishments. For more in-depth study, assign students to read a biography such as *Galileo and Experimental Science* by Rebecca B. Marcus.

Galileo was born and lived in Italy. He was a physicist and an astronomer, and he is credited with many scientific discoveries and inventions. Galileo created and used a telescope (adapted from the invention of the spy glass) to make observations of the solar system, and discovered sunspots, mountains and craters on the moon, the four largest moons of Jupiter, and the phases of Venus. As a physicist, he discovered the law of falling bodies, the law of the pendulum, and the motions of projectiles. Among his other accomplishments, Galileo built a thermoscope, constructed a geometrical and military compass, and devised a machine for raising water. All these endeavors required careful observation and measurement over a long period of time. Galileo kept detailed records to trace patterns in the natural world he studied. His careful data collection allowed him to make discoveries, find new applications of previously known principles, and invent many useful new tools.

During his youth Galileo contemplated various scientific ideas. He found fault with current scientific methods and presented his new ideas to less-than-enthusiastic audiences. Despite criticism, Galileo continued to advance his own ideas and discoveries. His devotion to his work, his belief in its importance, and the support of his daughter, Virginia, with whom he corresponded frequently after she became a nun in the Monastery of San Matteo, prevented him from giving in to his critics. He was determined to advance his controversial theories at any cost. As a professor, Galileo inspired a small, yet growing, number of students who studied with him.

Galileo's work required precise calculations and observations using less than ideal instruments. His many long hours spent diligently poring over astronomical charts, and writings, and observing the skies through his elementary telescopes, took their toll on his eyesight. Over the years his eyes began to fail; at the time of his death he was completely blind.

Galileo was scorned by fellow scientists, including Francis Bacon, for discoveries and assertions that contradicted Aristotle's theory that only perfectly spherical bodies could exist in the heavens and nothing new could be formed there, beliefs which had been widely accepted for almost two thousand years. Galileo was also criticized for his theories regarding hydrostatics (the physics of liquid).

Through his discoveries Galileo found support for the Copernican theory that the sun, not the earth, is at the center of the solar system, although a direct proof would not come until 1838, when better instruments became available. Despite the absence of direct proof, Galileo was so convinced of the Copernican theory that he began a campaign to spread it and to push the Roman Catholic Church to modify prevailing interpretations of scripture that seemed to contradict it. At that time, most scientific work was done in close connection with the Church because most academics and well-educated people were church officials. His insistence alienated some skeptics, who tried to have Galileo condemned by the church. Galileo's determined effort to convince the Pope of his theory, despite lack of proof, eventually led to a church decree forbidding him to "hold or defend" the theory. Diligently, he continued his work, and sixteen years later wrote his famous *Dialogue on the Two World System*, which did not technically violate the church's decree as he understood it, though it did violate the possibly fraudulent report on file with the Vatican. Again prompted by skeptics who took personal offence at Galileo's arguments, a second trial was held in which he was sentenced to remain silent about the theory for the rest of his life. Galileo spent the remainder of his days working quietly and persistently under house arrest near Florence. He died on January 8, 1642. His diligence paid off when his works gained official Church approval in 1741, and when, based on further evidence, the Church accepted the Copernican theory as fact in 1822. An official apology was issued for the mistaken condemnation of Galileo in 1992 by Pope John Paul II.

Awareness

Ask students to share what they already know about Galileo. (Limit the time to keep the class focused.)

Explain that Galileo was a scientist and mathematician during the Renaissance and that he made many discoveries that changed scientific thinking during that time. During the Renaissance people were just beginning to accept new ideas and discoveries about the world they lived in and many remained skeptical, believing that ideas and theories that had lasted for so long must be correct. Throughout his life Galileo struggled with those who held this viewpoint. They did not accept Galileo's new assertions and tried to prevent him from publicizing them. Galileo, however, devoted to astronomy and physics, diligently continued studying and experimenting.

Ask students to define the term *diligence* in their own words. Share with them the definition at the beginning of this lesson. Discuss the difference between diligence and perseverance.

Understanding

Discuss how the time period in which he lived had an effect on Galileo's life and work.

Ask students to list the ways that Galileo showed diligence, and create a "Top 5" list of ways he displayed this virtue.

Using the definition at the beginning of this lesson as a basis, ask students how they can show diligence in their daily lives. Examples may include finishing all of their homework once they have started, or working to finish a short story or complete a project that they have recently begun.

Ask students why being diligent (showing diligence) is important. How did Galileo benefit from his own diligence? How did other people benefit from Galileo's diligence? Brainstorm other examples of historical figures who showed diligence in their lives.

Share the following scenario with students, and ask them to answer the questions that follow (students may work in pairs to discuss their answers): You are looking for a job and find the following want ad in the newspaper: *Employee wanted for day shift, must be diligent.*

- **What personal qualities make an applicant attractive to an employer?**
- **What could you do to show a potential employer that you are a diligent person?**
- **How would a diligent person go about finding a job?**

Action

A diligence plan

Assign students to create a diligence plan. Ask them to write out a series of goals for diligently completing an upcoming task or project (e.g., "by Wednesday I will have an outline done, by Friday I will have page one written..." etc.). Then have students implement their plans.

Thank-you cards for diligent people

Have students identify a member of the school community who exemplifies diligence. Have students create appreciation cards for him or her. In the cards, students should explain why they feel that person is worthy of praise. What would happen if that person did not do his or her job?

Reflection

On the diligence challenge

Allow students to share their thoughts on the completion of the diligence plan. How difficult was it? What strategies did they use? What helped or hindered students in reaching their goals at each stage? What obstacles can stand in the way of diligence? Was the overall task made easier or harder by setting short-term goals? Ask students to reflect on the level of stress they felt and the quality of the project they completed. Remind students that Galileo remained diligent even in the face of opposition. It might have been easier for him to give up his work. Why do some people procrastinate or fail to complete projects they have undertaken?

On the benefits of diligence	Ask students to reflect futher on diligence.

- **When is it easy to be diligent? Difficult?**
- **What can we do to help ourselves act diligently?**
- **What are the benefits of being diligent?**
- **When was it difficult for Galileo to maintain diligence?**
- **What or who encouraged Galileo to forge ahead despite opposition?**

Bibliography

Galileo image from:
http://mech.postech.ac.kr/fluidmech/history/Galileo.html

For Students and Teachers

Marcus, R. B. *Galileo and Experimental Science*. New York: Franklin Watts, 1961.
A 123-page chapter book for students, *Galileo* provides in-depth information on the man's life and contributions. Dated, but useful for gaining background knowledge and insight into the era.

For Teachers

Galileo Galilei http://galileo.imss.firenze.it/museo/b/egalilg.html
Sobel, D. *Galileo's Daughter*. New York: Walker & Co., 1999.

It is our duty to make the best of our misfortunes and not to suffer passion to interfere with our interest and public good.

—George Washington

PERSEVERANCE

PERSEVERANCE: The habit of continuing a worthy task until it is completed, even when faced with unpleasant or difficult obstacles.

Deficiency: Inconstancy	PERSEVERANCE	Excess: Obstinacy

This lesson is intended to prompt students to internalize the virtue of perseverance, using the life of George Washington as an example. The biographical information provided serves as the background for the lesson, though greater study of Washington's life through a selected biography is essential.

BACKGROUND

The information below provides a brief biographical overview highlighting instances of Washington's perseverance. Assign students to read a biography such as *George Washington, Father of our Country* by Wendie C. Old to gain a greater understanding of the life of George Washington.

George Washington was born into a wealthy Virginia planter's family on February 22, 1732. As a young boy, he received an education typical for the sons of planters at the time: he studied reading, writing, mathematics, classics, and the rules of decorum. From his studies of Roman history, Washington learned of Cincinnatus, a Roman general who served his country valiantly, but wanted nothing more than to modestly return to his farm when his tour of duty was over. Washington admired Cincinnatus' integrity, courage, and modesty, and tried to model his own character after this historical hero. Young George was also very concerned with cultivating his manners. At age twelve, he diligently copied out 110 "Rules of Civility and Decent Behavior in Company and Conversation" from a contemporary guide, and set about attempting to conform to these rules. It was not always easy, but George persevered and soon found it natural to abide by rules such as "show nothing to your friend that might affright him" and "in the presence of others, sing not to yourself with a humming noise nor drum with your fingers or feet."

George's father, Augustine, died in 1743, and George went to live with his half-brother, Lawrence, at Lawrence's plantation, Mount Vernon. Lawrence became a surrogate father to George, and George was devoted to him until Lawrence's death from tuberculosis in 1752, upon which he inherited the plantation.

During the early colonial period, when England and France were competing for land in the Americas, Washington was a soldier in the British colonial army. On Halloween night, October 31, 1753, 21-year-old Washington had a dangerous task ahead of him. He was asked to travel to a place along the Ohio River where a group of French soldiers were stationed to deliver a warning letter to the French commander. The journey took three weeks, and Washington rode through torrential rains and heavy snowstorms before he reached the Ohio River in Pennsylvania. Washington delivered a letter from the Governor of Virginia and warned the French commander that his troops must leave the region. Failure to do so would result in battle. The French thought they had a right to the river because a Frenchman, La Salle, had discovered it. Furthermore, they were managing a successful fur trade with Indians along the river. The French did not want to surrender their location to the British and they intended to stop English families from settling along the river.

The French refused to pull back, and in response, Washington set up a camp at Fort Necessity, near the French-held territory at Fort Duquesne. On July 3, 1754 a battle ensued, and 600 French soldiers and 100 of their Native American allies forced Washington's force of 100 British regulars and 293 Virginian soldiers to surrender. The French took two British officers captive, but allowed the rest of the force, led by Washington, to retreat. After this, Washington knew that he had to lead his men back to Virginia to report on what occurred.

Because the rain was unrelenting, it took a nearly a month for Washington to carry the news of the battle back to the Governor of Virginia. When his horses became weak, he continued on foot. Washington and his travel companion spent a whole day building a raft that would carry them across the Allegheny River. Once across the river, he bought new horses and rode to Virginia. They did not arrive until January 11, 1754. Washington persevered through the treacherous conditions because he understood the importance of his mission, and was dedicated to carrying it out.

Another example of Washington's perseverance occurred 21 years later. The American colonists had declared independence from Britain and were raising an army for defense. On June 15, 1775, Washington was unanimously elected to command the Continental Army. Although he did not have extensive military training, Washington accepted the challenge. He had little to work with; the army was untrained and in need of organization before a confrontation with the British could be successful, and resources were scarce. Despite such obstacles, opposition, and setbacks, Washington maintained his dedication. He made the best of various situations and led his soldiers to persevere in the midst of hardship.

Harsh weather was one obstacle that plagued the Continental Army. When snow and freezing rain began to hit hard, soldiers without boots or shoes wrapped their bare feet in old rags to protect them against the elements. One night they were too tired to set up camp, so they slept on the frozen earth. Some soldiers could sleep on clean hay, and others slept on the damp dirt floors of huts. The temperatures often dipped below zero, and the men lacked warm clothing. Poor conditions led to widespread disease. Typhoid fever and smallpox killed more than 2,000 men. Washington and his men also faced terrible food shortages. Getting supplies to their camp at Valley Forge was nearly impossible and the lack of food led some soldiers to eat leather from old boots. Many soldiers subsisted on flour-and-water paste that was cooked over a fire. After four long months the worst was finally over for the men who had survived the terrible winter. Washington saw his soldiers through the tough times and strove to ease the devastating circumstances. He persevered through that winter and helped his soldiers do the same.

At the conclusion of the American Revolution, Washington was called on by his country once again—he was asked to leave Virginia to go to New York to be inaugurated as the first President of the United States. He was 57 years old. He had been unanimously chosen president, which meant the government could get started without debating over a leader. Washington loved his home at Mt. Vernon. He hated to leave the cherry trees, beautiful flowers, and crops, and he was apprehensive about taking on a position that had never been filled before in the history of the world. But he abided by his sense of duty and acted in accordance with what he felt was best for his country.

Accepting responsibilities as President of the United States was a tremendous challenge for Washington because he was assuming a position no one else had ever held. He had been chosen president by his peers, but the election had not been based on a popular vote, and he had a large republic to lead fairly. He had no predecessors to learn from and few guidelines for running the newly formed nation;

the Constitution had not even been written yet. Washington persevered, however, and served his term with great success. He faced tough challenges such as land disputes and problematic international relations. The ultimate question that rested on Washington's shoulders was whether the new nation could maintain its independence.

At the end of his first term, Washington was ready to retire. However, his colleagues, including Alexander Hamilton, convinced him to remain in office for a second term. Once again, Washington displayed perseverance by continuing in his post, even though he knew that there would be unpleasant and difficult times.

Awareness

Millions of Americans have enjoyed freedom and prosperity as a result of the sacrifices made by early leaders such as George Washington. The challenging situations that Washington encountered during his lifetime required courage, determination, loyalty, and perseverance. Although the obstacles met by Washington are uncommon in our country today, we all face challenges and difficult situations that require perseverance. By studying Washington's life we can learn how this virtue helps us achieve individual and collective goals.

Ask students to define *perseverance* in their own words. Then offer and discuss the definition at the beginning of the lesson.

Ask students for examples of ways they or someone they know has shown perseverance.

- **What are some ways we persevere in our everyday lives? What situations are unpleasant or difficult yet need to be completed?**
- **Why is it necessary to persevere? Why not give up when a task is difficult or unpleasant?**
- **When might perseverance turn into obstinacy? When is "giving up" okay?**

Understanding

George Washington showed great perseverance throughout his life, and as a result, he was able to lead colonists in the forming of a new nation. Discuss the specific ways Washington showed perseverance throughout his life. Ask students to give examples from the biography they have read. How might history have been different if Washington had given up when the "going got tough"? How did his perseverance affect others as individuals (for example, keeping his men alive) and the nation as a whole? In what ways may he have inspired others to forge ahead in their noble tasks?

Action

Physical perseverance challenge

Work with students to organize a charity event such as a dance-a-thon or a 5K fun run which students will need perseverance to complete, not only for achieving their goal on the day of the event, but also in planning for it. Family and community members can also be invited to participate.

Class-wide perseverance goals

Work together as a class to create a week-long or month-long goal for all students that demands perseverance. For example, students might set a goal for themselves and for the class to read a certain number of books by the end of the month, or a certain number of pages a week of a longer book. Discuss and identify potential obstacles and ways to overcome them on the way to achieving this goal.

Individual perseverance goals

Ask students to reflect on challenges they will face in the upcoming days and weeks. List ways they could persevere in order to get through them. For example: "I have an important test coming up in my worst subject. Therefore, I will study at least one hour each night for the next week so I will be prepared. When I get frustrated, I will take short breaks to help myself refocus." Other examples may include practicing a musical piece until it is mastered, vowing not to fight with a sibling for a week, completing all homework assignments on time for two weeks, or going to bed on time for an entire week.

Ask students to focus on one challenge and outline a specific plan for persevering to meet that challenge. (You may share your own challenge as an example.) The plan should include strategies for sticking with it. After their experience, students should write an essay explaining the results of their success or why they may have failed to persevere. What obstacles or setbacks did they face? Were these overcome? Why is it important to persevere to meet their goal?

Reflection

On the physical perseverance challenge

Discuss the results of the physical perseverance challenge.

- **Did you accurately anticipate the difficulty of the activity?**
- **What did you think when dancing/running started to become unpleasant?**
- **What did you do or think to help yourself persevere?**
- **Did watching everyone else dance/run have an influence on you? Would you have given in more quickly if everyone was blindfolded and no one knew who was sitting down?**
- **If there was no external incentive for continuing to dance or run, would you have sat down sooner? If there was an award for the person who persevered the longest, would you have held out longer?**
- **What might have helped George Washington to persevere?**

Ask students to consider what effect other people may have had on Washington's ability to persevere. Then ask:

- **When is it easier to persevere? When is it more difficult?**
- **If someone is counting on you, how does it affect your ability to persevere?**
- **To what extent does your goal determine your ability to persevere?**

On the class perseverance goal

Encourage discussion about perseverance by asking the following questions:

- **What was the benefit of your perseverance? What was the sacrifice?**
- **What obstacles did you face while trying to persevere?**
- **What is the difference between an individual goal and a collective (group) goal for perseverance? How was this collective goal like certain of Washington's goals?**
- **How did you feel about the group challenge? What did you do to help your classmates persevere?**
- **What did you do to help yourself persevere?**

On the individual perseverance goals

At the end of the challenge, ask students to revisit their original goal and record the progress made. Share the results of your own challenge as an example. Encourage students to think of what they might do differently next time in order to be more successful. Ask students if it was difficult to persevere. What were some unanticipated obstacles? How did they feel about their success or lack of success? Encourage students to persevere until their goal is achieved.

Bibliography

For Students and Teachers

Egger-Bovet, H., et al. *US Kids History: Book of the American Colonies*. Boston: Little, Brown, 1996.

George Washington's Mount Vernon. http://www.mountvernon.org/

Marin, A. *George Washington and the Founding of a Nation*. New York: Dutton, 2001.

Old, W. C. *George Washington, Father of our Country*. Springfield, N.J.: Enslow, 1997.

Washington, George
http://search.biography.com/print_record.pl?id=20538

George Washington: A National Treasure
http://www.georgewashington.si.edu

The Crossing. A&E Home Video, 2000.

Metropolitan Museum of Art. Leutze's *George Washington Crossing the Delaware*. www.metmuseum.org/explore/gw/el_gw.htm
This site focuses on a great artistic representation of one instance demonstrating Washington's perseverance: his crossing of the Delaware River on Christmas Eve to stage a surprise attack of Hessian mercenaries stationed in Trenton, New Jersey. This site focuses on the art-related aspects of Emanuel Leutze's famous painting, but the two websites listed in the section below focus on integrating art and history.

For Teachers

Brookhiser, R. *Founding Father: Rediscovering Geoge Washington*. New York: The Free Press, 1996.

Jaffe, I. *George Washington Crossing the Delaware*.
www.npr.org/programs/
morning/features/patc/georgewashington.

Washington Crossing the Delaware.
www.americanrevolution.org/delxone.html.

CITIZENSHIP

CITIZENSHIP: Taking action that shows pride in one's country and its people; acting on behalf of one's fellow citizens for the good of the country.

Deficiency: Indifference	CITIZENSHIP	Excess: Blind Allegiance

John Adams was a dedicated statesman recognized for his great patriotism. The following lesson is designed to focus on John Adams's life of citizenship while prompting students to explore the virtue of citizenship in their own lives.

BACKGROUND

The following biographical information serves as a short description of the life of John Adams. It is suggested that students read *John Adams: Second President of the United States* by Marlene Targ Brill or another biographical work before beginning this lesson.

Besides being one of the founders of our nation and our second President, John Adams was also a farmer, a lawyer, a legislator, a diplomat, the Vice President, and a father. The story of his life chronicles an admirable record of service to his country and to his fellow citizens.

John Adams was born on October 30, 1735 in the North Precinct of Braintree in the Massachusetts Bay Colony (now Quincy, Mass.), a member of the fourth generation of Adamses of the American colonies. His parents, John Adams and Susanna Boylston Adams, were prominent citizens of their community; his father was a church deacon and town selectman. As a boy, Adams greatly admired his father, an

Our obligations to our country never cease but with our lives.

—John Adams

honest, upright man with an independent streak; in fact, his only ambition for the future was to become a farmer like his father. Although his education and opportunity led him to law and politics, he remained inspired by his father's example throughout his life.

After graduating from Harvard College and teaching for a brief time, Adams began to study law as a clerk in Worcester, Mass., and in 1758 was admitted to the Suffolk County Bar. As a young lawyer, Adams became renowned for his gifts of elocution and elegant writing. He became involved in the early stages of the movement for independence. He served on the Massachusetts delegations to both the First and Second Continental Congresses and on the committee to draft the Declaration of Independence.

During the Revolutionary War, Adams went to France and the Netherlands on diplomatic missions; he ultimately served with Benjamin Franklin, Thomas Jefferson, John Jay, and Henry Laurens on the committee to negotiate treaties of peace and commerce with England. In 1785, he became minister to the Court of St. James, where he served until 1788. He returned to the United States and was elected Vice President under President George Washington.

After two terms as Vice President, John Adams became the second President of the United States in 1796, narrowly defeating Thomas Jefferson. It was a time of tension both at home and abroad. During his presidency, Adams had to contend with the rapidly increasing friction between the two political parties, the Federalists (Adams' party) and the Republicans, while trying to avert involvement in the war between England and France. The next presidential election was also a close race— but this time victory was Jefferson's.

After leaving the presidency, Adams retired to his home in Braintree, where he resumed his friendship and fascinating correspondence with Thomas Jefferson. On July 4, 1826, the fiftieth anniversary of the Declaration of Independence, John Adams died. Among his last words were "Thomas Jefferson survives." But Jefferson had, in fact, died at Monticello only a few hours before.

Awareness | Ask students to define *citizenship* in their own words and to brainstorm a list of activities associated with citizenship. Divide and categorize this list (some categories might include: individual responsibilities, social responsibilities, etc.). Discuss the definitions provided at the beginning of this lesson. Ask students to explain how their ideas relate to these definitions of citizenship. Then discuss the rights and responsibilities of United States citizens.

Understanding | Using Marlene Targ Brill's biography of Adams, *John Adams: Second President of the United States* from the *Encyclopedia of Presidents* series, to provide specific examples, have students recount the specific ways that John Adams showed citizenship.

Ask students to brainstorm ways that they can practice citizenship in their daily lives. Help students to realize that citizenship need not mean fighting in a war or denouncing another country. It involves positively supporting one's own country. Participating in Memorial Day services, displaying an American flag, cleaning up a neighborhood park, and helping the homeless are examples of activities that display one's citizenship.

Ask students who are citizens of other countries to give examples of how people in other nations demonstrate citizenship by showing support for their country or leaders.

Ask students to analyze the following words of John Adams that have been "quoted for generations within the Adams family and beyond" (McCullough, p. 236):

I must study politics and war that my sons may have liberty to study mathematics and philosophy. My sons ought to study mathematics and philosophy, geography, natural history, naval architecture, navigation, commerce, and agriculture in order to give their children a right to study paintings, poetry, music, architecture, statuary, tapestry, and porcelain.

- **Adams felt a great responsibility for creating a new nation. How does this quote reflect that responsibility?**
- **What is Adams suggesting about the progress of a nation or a society?**
- **How is this progress related to citizenship? How is this progress related to education? How are education and citizenship related?**

Discuss with students the choice made by Adams in the aftermath of a critical event:

To the surprise of all who recognized Adams for his dedication to the patriots, he agreed to defend the British soldiers on trial for their part in the conflict known as the Boston Massacre in 1770 (see Paul Revere's famous engraving of the incident, left). The soldiers had fired on a crowd of rioting men and boys who were throwing rocks, sticks, snow, and ice, leaving three men dead. When no one would agree to represent the soldiers, Adams stepped in, firmly believing that everyone, no matter who they were, deserved a fair trial.

Because of his decision, he suffered derision and public outrage, causing him to fear for his safety and the safety of his family. After the trial, he said that he also lost more than half of his legal clients (McCullough, p. 68).

- **Adams's famous cousin, the great patriot Sam Adams, apparently did not try to dissuade John Adams from taking the soldiers' case. David McCullough surmises that it was possible that "Sam Adams had privately approved, even encouraged it behind the scenes, out of respect for John's fierce integrity, and on the theory that so staunch a show of fairness would be good politics." Why would Sam Adams believe that John Adams' decision was a good one for the patriot cause?**

- **What is integrity? How did John Adams show integrity in making the decision to defend the British soldiers?**

Ask students to examine Adams's dishonorable actions:

As with many great leaders, John Adams's stellar record of service to his country is not entirely without blemish. As President, he endorsed the Alien and Sedition Acts of 1798, bills meant to prevent acts of subversion against the government. One of these acts called for the imposition of harsh penalties for those who had the audacity to criticize the government. As a result, a large number of journalists were jailed for the publication of articles in which they voiced their dissent. (http://gi.grolier.com/presidents/ea/bios/02pjohn.html)

These laws were seen as necessary in the face of war with France, and although they were not applied to the letter, clearly they are against the Constitution and the rights of American citizens.[1]

> • **Keeping in mind what you know of John Adams and his commitment to his country, what reasons do you think he would give to support the Alien and Sedition Acts?**
> • **How might fear cause people to compromise their principles?**

Action

Memorial visit

Take the class on a walking field trip to a cemetery or soldiers' memorial. Bring American flags and/or flowers to leave at the graves of men and women who died defending their country. Explain to students that by recognizing the people who died for the well-being of our nation, we are taking pride in those honorable deeds and recognizing the value of our freedom and protection.

The American flag

Analyze the symbolism of the American flag (ask students from other countries to explain the symbolism of their countries' flags) and discuss why countries have flags. Help students understand the progression of the modification of the original U.S. flag designed for the 13 colonies. Helpful resources include the Betsy Ross homepage at www.ushistory.org/betsy, the Flag of the United States website at www.usflag.org, and, for information on all types of flags, the Flags of the World website at http://flagspot.net/flags. (This activity may also be completed using the state flag.) Then develop a class flag using symbols of pride and loyalty to your class, grade, or school.

Respect for the flag

Explain to students that the flag is a symbol of our country and treating it with the utmost respect is a way of showing loyalty and citizenship. Teach students the proper way to fold a flag. Also explain proper treatment of a flag: never letting it touch the ground, not throwing it away when it gets old, when to fly it at half-staff, etc. (See www.usflag.org/flag.etiquette.html.)

---

[1]The first amendment to the Constitution states: "Congress shall make no law respecting an establishment of religion, or prohibiting the free exercise thereof, or abridging the freedom of speech, or of the press; or the right of the people peaceably to assemble, and to petition the government for a redress of grievances." The Alien and Sedition Acts were in direct opposition to freedom of speech and the press, and the right of citizens to "petition the government for a redress of grievances."

The Pledge of Allegiance	Give each student a copy of the Pledge of Allegiance (reproducible page), written in 1892 by Francis Bellamy in honor of the nation's first Columbus Day celebration. Because it is so often memorized and recited without analysis of meaning or content, it is important for students to analyze the language and origin of terms such as "indivisible" and "allegiance." Note recent arguments and developments regarding the wording of the pledge, especially the phrase "under God." Then ask:

- **When do we recite the Pledge?**
- **Why is it important?**
- **What does it symbolize?**

(This activity may also be modified and done with the National Anthem. Older students can analyze the Bill of Rights, the Declaration of Independence, and/or the preamble to the Constitution of the United States.)

Citizenship challenge	Have students set practical goals to help them become better citizens themselves, in school or in their neighborhoods. Ask students to undertake at least one activity that shows their citizenship (for example, volunteering to help at a homeless shelter or to clean up a section of the playground or neighborhood). Allow time for students to reflect frequently (in writing, through presentation, or in discussion with a partner) on how successful they are at meeting these goals.
Reflection *On the memorial visit*	Ask students to write an essay in which they reflect on their experiences at the cemetery or memorial. What were their thoughts? What aspect of citizenship did they appreciate the most? How has this unit shaped their understanding of what citizenship means?
A tribute to Adams	Ask students to select specific examples of John Adams's citizenship (quotes, illustrations, etc.) and create a tribute in the form of an original poem, a collage, or a video about these acts. Have students write an essay explaining why they selected those specific examples and how those examples demonstrate Adams's citizenship. Give students the opportunity to view each other's projects.

On the citizenship challenge	Ask students to describe their experiences in attempting to reach their goals to become better citizens. Were they successful? Why? Why not? Are there goals that still need to be met? What new goals could they set?
Good citizens today	Ask students to identify someone who is a good citizen within the school. Identify what makes that person a good citizen; provide examples of that person's actions. As a class, write a letter or tribute to this individual that points out his/her actions of good citizenship. Have students present their letters or tributes to the good citizens they selected.

Bibliography

For Teachers

McCullough, D. *John Adams*. New York: Simon and Schuster, 2001.

For Students and Teachers

Biographies of John and Abigail Adams—White House webpage
www.whitehouse.gov/history/presidents/ja2.html

The Adams Family Papers—An Electronic Archive.
www.masshist.org

Adams National Historical Park, Quincy, Mass.
www.nps.gov/adam

Brill, M. T. *John Adams: Second President of the United States (Encyclopedia of Presidents)*. New York: Children's Press, 1987.

Harness, C. *The Revolutionary John Adams*. National Geographic, 2003.

Recommended Film

1776. Directed by Peter H. Hunt and starring William Daniels and Howard DaSilva, 1972.

THE PLEDGE OF ALLEGIANCE

I Pledge Allegiance to the flag
of the United States of America
and to the Republic
for which it stands,
one Nation (under God), indivisible, with
liberty and justice for all.

Nobody ever helps me into carriages, or over mud-puddles, or gives me any best place! And ain't I a woman?

—Sojourner Truth

COURAGE

COURAGE: The ability to face and endure what is dangerous, difficult, or painful; knowing what is to be feared and what is not to be feared, and acting accordingly (Aristotle).

Deficiency: **Cowardice**	—	**COURAGE**	—	Excess: **Recklessness**

This lesson is intended to teach students about courage, help them reflect on this virtue in their daily lives, and introduce them to an exemplary person of courage. Ideally, students should be aware of the social and political climate of the early nineteenth century, and will have studied slavery, the Emancipation Act, and other related topics before this lesson is introduced. This lesson may also be adapted to correspond with the study of slavery, women's rights, and African-American leaders.

BACKGROUND

The following biographical information serves as a short description of the life of Sojourner Truth. It is suggested that students read *Sojourner Truth and the Struggle for Freedom* by Edward Beecher Claflin before beginning this lesson.

Sojourner Truth was a strong proponent of equal rights for all African-American women. Born a slave in 1797 with the name Isabella Baumfree, Truth grew to be nearly six feet tall by the age of thirteen. As a young girl, Truth was sold to a master who beat her with rods that had been heated in the fire. She was sold several times during her life, and eventually married a slave named Thomas with whom she had five children. After the Missouri Compromise of 1820 outlawed slavery north of the line of latitude running along 36'30", Truth learned that her five-year-old son, who was born in New York and thus according to the new law should be freed on his twenty-first birthday, had been illegally sold to someone in the South. She desperately wanted her son back, and courageously filed suit to have him returned. She was the first black woman ever to sue a white man and win.

Truth had a strong faith in God, and she shared her beliefs about religion and social injustice with others. She adopted the name Sojourner Truth when she began to travel ("sojourn" means to wander or travel), preaching what she believed to be the truth. Truth fought for equal rights for women and African-Americans. She gave her most famous speech at the Women's Rights Conference in Akron, Ohio, in 1851. Truth boldly stood up and argued "Ain't I a woman?" to a crowd of people who said that women were not intelligent enough to vote and who denied them equal rights. Truth stood up for what she believed in and courageously expressed her convictions.

Although Sojourner Truth never learned to read or write, she was an advocate for equality throughout her life. She continued to travel and speak to audiences. She even corresponded with and met President Lincoln, who was already familiar with her speeches. Like Lincoln, she courageously confronted the injustice that surrounded her.

Awareness | Write the words "courage" and "recklessness" on the board. Ask students to list actions that they associate with each term. Have students list situations that require courage. Discuss the relationship between fear and courage, and why both recklessness and cowardice "miss the mark." What are some disadvantages and dangers of not having enough fear (recklessness)?

Understanding | Discuss the life of Sojourner Truth. Use the following questions as a guide.

- **What do Truth's actions tell you about her priorities and beliefs?**
- **What does it mean to have courage or to be courageous? (Refer to the definition of courage on the opening page.)**
- **When specifically did Truth display courage? Give examples.**
- **What might Truth have feared? What was dangerous or difficult about what she did?**
- **What obstacles did she have to overcome? What risks did she face?**
- **What positive outcomes was she seeking? What were her motivations?**
- **Why were her actions seen as courageous and not reckless?**

Sojourner Truth needed courage to stand up against slavery and inequality. Ask the following questions to connect the discussion of courage to students' lives.

- **What are some challenges that young people face today?**
- **How does courage help young people make wise choices?**
- **What do you need courage for in your everyday life?**
- **What special circumstances require courage?**
- **How might you show courage in those situations?**

Discuss the saying, "What is right is not always popular, and what is popular is not always right." Help students realize that it takes courage to:

- speak out for something you think is right even if it is an unpopular choice among friends.
- ask someone for forgiveness when you've done something wrong.

- welcome new people or remain open to new situations.
- admit when you need help with something.
- resist what you know is harmful (e.g., drugs and alcohol) even if others around you are indulging in them.
- find a way to confront a friend about a difficult topic such as drug use.

Action

"Ain't I a Woman?" speech

Share with students Sojourner Truth's "Ain't I a Woman?" speech (included at the end of this lesson). Ask two students to practice and then deliver the narrated version. One student should narrate the descriptions of the audience's reactions while the other reads the speech.

Public speaking

Truth was able to express her ideas and frustrations to people in an effective way because she was a powerful speaker. It is important for us to be able to articulate our thoughts and deliver them clearly to others. This activity is intended to help students find the courage to confront and overcome their fears of public speaking.

Ask students to write original persuasive speeches about courage. You may give students quotes or phrases about courage that may be used as openers. Subtopics may include:

- an original speech that pays tribute to Sojourner for her courage
- how to summon courage in a particular situation
- why it is necessary for middle school students to have courage
- how we can learn about courage from Truth's example (or someone else's)

Discuss with students the criteria of an effective speech, using "Ain't I a Woman" as an example. Allow class time for all students to deliver their speeches.

Role-plays	Ask students to discuss with a partner or reflect individually on the ways they summon courage in difficult situations. Then ask for volunteers to share their ideas with the class. How do they act courageously when they are met with peer pressure? Ask students to act out these situations in role-plays. Help students recognize that they all have the courage to face any of these situations, and that the challenge is to summon the courage from within themselves. This usually comes with practice, as Aristotle reminds us, we "become brave by doing brave acts." (Nicomachean Ethics, II.1) Identify a situation in which the students might need to demonstrate courage on a daily basis. Have students practice one act of courage each day for a week.
Courage interviews	Ask students to interview a member of the school or local community who exemplifies courage. Identify specific challenges in the person's life and how they faced these challenges courageously.
Courage field trip	Take students on a field trip to a firehouse or police station. Interview the firefighters or police officers. What factors motivate them and their collegues to risk their lives for others?

Reflection

Ask students the following questions regarding Truth's speech.

On the "Ain't I a Woman" speech

- **What reactions did Truth receive?**
- **What point is she trying to make?**
- **What is she saying about equality?**
- **What is a double standard? What double standards does Truth point out?**

On public speaking

Prompt students to reflect on the pressures of delivering a speech. Ask volunteers to share some of their worries or apprehensions.

- **Were you nervous about giving your speech? Why?**
- **How did you find the courage you needed?**
- **What advice would you give to someone who needed courage to perform?**
- **Are these the same obstacles that Truth needed to overcome? Why or why not?**
- **What added pressures did she need courage to face?**

On the application of courage	Ask students to write a short essay reflecting on a time in their lives that required great courage. Students should discuss why the situation required courage, how they handled it, how they were able to find/summon courage, what may have happened if they had not been courageous, and what the outcome of their courageous action was.
On a courageous life	Have students imagine that the year is 2075. A journalist has been asked to write an article about the student's life, entitled "A Courageous Life." Have students write the article and describe a situation in which they would have demonstrated great courage in their lives. The situation could be something that has already occurred, or something they imagine happening in the future.

Bibliography

Truth Image from: http://tlc.ai.org/truthsoj.htm

For Students and Teachers

Claflin, E. B. *Sojourner Truth and the Struggle for Freedom*. New York: Barrons, 1987.
This biographical account of Truth's life is written for students from ages 10 to 13 and provides insight into her experiences as a slave and as a civil rights advocate. The 142-page chapter book chronicles her struggles and heroic strength by explaining how she was bought and sold, finally freed, and stood up for the rights of women and blacks.

Whalin, W. T. *Sojourner Truth, American Abolitionist*. Philadelphia: Chelsea House, 1999.
A more challenging read, but an in-depth account of Truth's life, including review of the pressing issues of the time period.
A 195-page chapter book.

Sojourner Truth http://www.lkwdpl.org/wihohio/trut-soj.htm

For Teachers

Gilbert, O. *Narrative of Sojourner Truth*.
http://digital.library.upenn.edu/women/truth/ 1850/1850.html

This site contains the full text of an 1850 account of the life of Sojourner Truth as dictated by Truth herself. Although written in 1850, it is still readable and interesting today. Many of the anecdotes described in the text could even be taken as excepts and used with students.

Modern History Sourcebook: Sojourner Truth: Ain't I a Woman?
http://www.fordham.edu/halsall/mod/sojtruth2.html

The Max Warburg Courage Curriculum. http://www.maxcourage.org/

Ain't I a Woman? (abridged, text version)

That man over there says that women need to be helped into carriages, and lifted over ditches, and have the best place everywhere. Nobody ever helps me into carriages, or over mud-puddles, or gives me any best place! And ain't I a woman?

Look at me! Look at my arm! I have ploughed and planted, and gathered into barns, and no man could head me! And ain't I a woman? I could work as much and eat as much as a man—when I could get it—and bear the lash as well! And ain't I a woman?

I have borne thirteen children, and seen most all sold off to slavery, and when I cried out with my mother's grief, none but Jesus heard me! And ain't I a woman?

Obliged to you for hearing me, and now old Sojourner ain't got nothing more to say.

Ain't I a Woman?[1] (narrated version)

The tumult subsided at once, and every eye was fixed on this almost Amazon form, which stood nearly six feet high, head erect, and eyes piercing the upper air like one in a dream. At her first word there was a profound hush. She spoke in deep tones, which, though not loud, reached every ear in the house, and away through the throng at the doors and windows.

"Dat man ober dar say dat womin needs to be helped into carriages, and lifted ober ditches, and to hab de best place everywhar. Nobody eber helps me into carriages, or ober mud-puddles, or gibs me any best place!" *And raising herself to her full height, and her voice to a pitch like rolling thunder, she asked,* "And a'n't I a woman? Look at me! Look at my arm! *(And she bared her right arm to the shoulder, showing her tremendous muscular power.)* I have ploughed, and planted, and gathered into barns, and no man could head me! And a'n't I a woman? I could work as much and eat as much as a man—when I could get it—and bear de lash as well! And a'n't I a woman? I have borne thirteen chilern, and seen 'em mos' all sold off to slavery, and when I cried out with my mother's grief, none but Jesus heard me! And a'n't I a woman?

"Den dey talks 'bout dis ting in de head; what dis dey call it?" *("Intellect," whispered someone near.)* "Dat's it, honey. What's dat got to do wid womin's rights or nigger's rights? If my cup won't hold but a pint, and yourn holds a quart, wouldn't ye be mean not to let me have my little half-measure full?"

And she pointed her significant finger, and sent a keen glance at the minister who had made the argument. The cheering was long and loud.

"Den dat little man in black dar, he say women can't have as much rights as men, 'cause Christ wan't a woman! Whar did your Christ come from?"

Rolling thunder couldn't have stilled that crowd, as did those deep, wonderful tones, as she stood there with outstretched arms and eyes of fire. Raising her voice still louder, she repeated,

"Whar did your Christ come from? From God and a woman! Man had nothin' to do wid Him."

Oh, what a rebuke that was to that little man.

---

[1]http://www.fordham.edu/halsall/mod/sojtruth2.html

Turning again to another objector, she took up the defense of Mother Eve. I can not follow her through it all. It was pointed, and witty, and solemn; eliciting at almost every sentence deafening applause; and she ended by asserting:

"If de fust woman God ever made was strong enough to turn de world upside down all alone, dese women togedder [and she glanced her eye over the platform] ought to be able to turn it back, and get it right side up again! And now dey is asking to do it, de men better let 'em."

Long continued cheering greeted this.

"'Bleeged to ye for hearin' on me, and now ole Sojourner han't got nothin' more to say."

Amid roars of applause, she returned to her corner, leaving more than one of us with streaming eyes, and hearts beating with gratitude.

With malice toward none; with charity for all; with firmness in the right, as God gives us to see the right, let us strive on to finish the work we are in; to bind up the nation's wounds; to care for him who shall have borne the battle, and for his widow, and his orphan—to do all which may achieve and cherish a just, and a lasting peace, among ourselves, and with all nations.

—Abraham Lincoln, Second Inaugural Address

JUSTICE

JUSTICE: Sound reason, righteousness, and fairness in relation to ourselves and others.

> ## JUSTICE*

*Justice is a virtue that does not fall along a mean. A person can certainly be unjust, which would indicate a deficiency of justice. However, the nature of justice is that a person can never be too just or fair; therefore, an excess of this virtue does not exist.

During their studies of the American Civil War, students will study the life of Abraham Lincoln, whose moral conviction provides a model for a life of virtue. Students should have studied the events leading up to the Civil War and should be aware of the dire state of the nation that awaited Lincoln when he took his oath of office in 1860. Despite fierce opposition from the South, Lincoln consistently made choices based on sound moral principles and pulled the divided Union back together.

BACKGROUND

The following biographical information serves as a short description of the life of Abraham Lincoln. It is suggested that students read *Lincoln: A Photobiography* by Russell Freedman or another biographical work before beginning this lesson.

Many of the stories from Abraham Lincoln's childhood have become American legends. Lincoln is often dubbed "Honest Abe," but honesty is simply the foundation on which he based a life committed to justice.

Abraham Lincoln grew up in a log cabin in Kentucky in a poor, uneducated, yet loving family. He developed an insatiable appetite for reading by listening to Bible passages that were read to him at home. His career as a student was brief, however, and he wanted to learn more. He borrowed books from neighbors and read *Pilgrim's Progress*, *Aesop's Fables*, *Arabian Nights*, and *Robinson Crusoe*. According to legend, when he borrowed *Life of Washington*, and it became ruined from rain, Lincoln worked for his neighbor until the book's worth had been paid off. As he grew older he discovered a love of Shakespeare, especially the play *MacBeth*[1]. Even as President of the U.S. he often passed the time he spent traveling around the country by reading and reflecting on Shakespeare's plays.

As a boy and young man, Lincoln helped his father on the farm. When he grew older, he worked as a railsplitter to earn some change for himself. The Lincoln family moved to Indiana and then to Illinois. Young Abe decided to head out alone to New Salem, Ill., where he found a job in a store. It is said that he once discovered that he had shortchanged a customer without either of them realizing it, so he walked several miles to return the few cents. Eventually, the store failed, and Lincoln decided to run for the Illinois state legislature. Although his reputation as a good speaker and his honesty and humor were rapidly gaining him popularity, he lost the election. Fortunately, he did not give up; he worked hard, ran again, and this time was elected. In the meantime, he fought to overcome his meager education by studying to become a lawyer. He also met and married Mary Ann Todd, a young woman from Kentucky with whom he eventually had four sons.

Lincoln practiced his speaking skills during his years as a lawyer and became well known for his quick wit. He was elected to the U.S. House of Representatives, where he was forced to take a stand on the slavery issue. Lincoln said that he had always hated slavery. He spoke out against the Dred Scott decision, which announced that slaves had always been the property of white men and that they were not entitled to be citizens. Soon Lincoln was nominated to run against Stephen Douglas for a seat in the U.S. Senate. Lincoln was a former Whig, now a Republican, and opposed slavery. Douglas was a Democrat and an ardent supporter of slavery. Lincoln kicked off his campaign by informing his supporters that the country could not survive in its present state. "A house divided against itself cannot stand," he proclaimed. "I believe this government cannot endure permanently half slave and half free. I do not expect the Union to be dissolved—I do not expect the house to fall—but I do expect it will cease to be divided. It will become all one thing, or all the other."

In July of 1858, Lincoln challenged Douglas to a series of debates. It must have been a fascinating sight to see "Long Abe," as people called him, over six feet tall in an

---

[1]Beran, Michael Knox. "Lincoln, *MacBeth*, and the Moral Imagination: *Humanitas*, Volume XI, No. 2, 1998.

ill-fitting, rumpled suit, standing next to Senator Douglas, dubbed "the Little Giant," barely five feet four inches tall, who traveled in high style and had an aggressive manner. Audiences sat and attentively listened to them debate the slavery issue. Despite his magnificent orating skills and his ability to attract supporters, Lincoln lost the election. He was walking home in the rain when he heard the news, and he lost his footing. He regained his balance and said, "It was a slip, not a fall." He was right; two years later he won the presidential election over Stephen Douglas. By the time Lincoln took office, he had a national crisis waiting for him. Seven Southern states, enraged by the election of the anti-slavery candidate, had seceded from the Union.

Lincoln rode into Washington to deliver his inaugural address on March 4, 1861. Only a month later, the rebels opened fire on Fort Sumter, and the American Civil War began. The new president had to cope with tremendous frustrations in trying to mobilize the Union army against the determined Confederate soldiers. General George McClellan, who commanded the Union army, probably gave up several victories because of his tendency to hesitate and to pull back his men at the crucial moment. An impatient Lincoln wrote to him, "Dear General, if you do not want to use the army, I would like to borrow it for a few days." He went to meet with McClellan after the battle of Antietam and sent him home. General McClellan responded, "They have made a great mistake. Alas for my poor country!"

While waiting for the Union troops to mobilize, Lincoln attacked the slavery issue again. On January 1, 1863, he signed the Emancipation Proclamation, a document that freed the slaves in the rebel territories. "If my name ever goes into history," the president said, "it will be for this act."

President Lincoln was not without his share of personal hardships during his years in office. In 1862, his son Willie died from typhoid fever. The Lincolns took the loss especially hard because only twelve years earlier, their three-year-old son Eddie had died.

After the battle of Gettysburg, President Lincoln gave a speech to dedicate the battlefield to the soldiers who had died while fighting. The Gettysburg Address is now one of the most famous speeches in all of American history. Shortly after Lincoln gave this speech, Richmond fell to the Union army and the North went wild with excitement. Lincoln was equally overjoyed and on April 3, 1865 he said, "Thank God I have lived to see this. It seems to me that I have been dreaming a horrid nightmare for four years, and now the nightmare is gone. I want to see Richmond." As he made his way through the wreck and ruin of the city, people came to meet Lincoln, to see him and to touch him, because they knew that he was the man who had steadfastly worked on their and the nation's behalf.

Lincoln was delighted, because he knew the Union would be preserved. However, his jovial mood was unfortunately to come to a sudden end. Less than two weeks after his triumphant walk through Richmond, on April 15, 1865, Lincoln was assassinated at Ford's Theater by John Wilkes Booth, a Confederate supporter who hated Lincoln and the North for their victory.

Attached to this lesson are the texts of the Emancipation Proclamation, Lincoln's "A House Divided" speech, and his Second Inaugural Address. Teachers may use these documents to supplement this lesson.

Awareness

Write the definition of *justice* found at the beginning of this lesson on the board. Ask students to "translate" this definition in a way that relates to their own lives. What does justice mean for us? How do we show justice? Ask students to list examples of ways Abraham Lincoln demonstrated justice in his personal and political life.

Understanding

Lincoln: A Photobiography by Russell Freedman provides a remarkable account of Lincoln's life from his birth until his assassination. It delves into the personal as well as public trials he endured and is explicit in revealing "Honest Abe's" moral character. Draw students' attention to anecdotes from Lincoln's early life that reveal his honesty and sense of justice. Ask them to identify and discuss his policies during the Civil War that show his moral conviction as well.

Cultivate further understanding of Abraham Lincoln's character by introducing the Lincoln-Douglas debates and the two candidates' opposing views on slavery. Present these two quotes to the class, both of which come from the debate at Ottawa on August 21, 1858:

> *This government was instituted to secure the blessings of freedom. Slavery is an unqualified evil to the Negro, to the white man, to the soil, and to the State.*
>
> **—Abraham Lincoln**

> *I am opposed to Negro equality. I believe this government was made by the white man for the white man to be administered by the white man.*
>
> **—Stephen Douglas**

Discuss the meaning of each quote. To what popular beliefs of the pre-Civil War era do you attribute each candidate's opinion about the rights of slaves? What does each opinion say about the speaker's character? Lincoln's inclination to do the right thing with respect to other people is revealed by his belief in the assertion of the Declaration of Independence that "all men are created equal" and by his fight to preserve the Union. We call Lincoln's virtue *justice* or *rectitude*. Using the differing opinions on slavery as the context, discuss whether what is right can change according to popular opinion, or whether there is a universal standard of right. (For more information on the Lincoln-Douglas debates, see http://mkoehler.msu.edu/MattWeb/courses/CEP_909_FA02/Civil War/Politics_Debates.asp)

Action
The Gettysburg Address

Ask students to memorize the Gettysburg Address and recite it in front of the class. Explain the significance of committing such an important speech to memory. The Gettysburg Address reflects Lincoln's commitment to the preservation of the Union and his belief in equality for *all* Americans.

A justice challenge

For one week, challenge students to treat everyone with the same respect that Lincoln believed all human beings deserved. This lesson may provide a good opportunity to address the problem of bullying in a middle school. Discuss the right course of action to take if a student sees someone being bullied, even though the right thing to do may not be easy. For instance, a student who witnesses the bullying should speak up or seek the help of a teacher, but not stand by passively. Select a time limit to carry out the challenge and put it into action.

Role-plays

Brainstorm situations from students' own lives in which they witness injustice. Why is injustice so harmful? How can it be overcome? Ask students to write role-plays in which they act out a situation that requires just action. Students may perform the appropriate act of justice or pause to let classmates discuss possible solutions.

Reflection

On presidential qualities

Have students write a one- to two-page essay in response to *Lincoln: A Photobiography*, in which they address the following questions:

- **When you are old enough to vote in four or five years, what qualities will you look for in a president?**
- **Does your knowledge of Abraham Lincoln's life change your thinking about the qualities that are important in a strong leader?**

On the Gettysburg Address

Have students write a short essay (in class, 20-30 minutes) on what the Gettysburg Address means to them. Students should answer the following questions:

- **What were the challenges and benefits of memorizing the address?**
- **What was the purpose of memorizing it?**
- **How does it reveal Lincoln's own justice?**

On the justice challenge

Have students write about their experiences during the classroom challenge. Students should answer the following questions:

- **Was it easy to try to do the right thing? Why or why not?**
- **Did you find it a worthwhile experience, or was it cumbersome?**
- **What were the advantages and disadvantages to achieving the goal?**
- **Why was your action the right thing to do?**
- **Did you have any experiences in which Lincoln's life might serve as an example for how to make a decision or how to behave?**

On the role-plays

Have students write a one-page essay in which they answer the following:

- **Was it difficult to come up with a scenario for your role-play? Why or why not?**
- **Was it difficult to come up with a just solution to the scenarios presented? Why or why not?**
- **In what way do justice and injustice impact your daily life?**

Bibliography

Lincoln image from: holydays.tripod.com/linc.htm

For Students and Teachers

Abraham Lincoln Research Site
http://members.aol.com/RVSNorton/Lincoln2.html
This is an excellent site for both students and teachers. It contains volumes of information on Abraham Lincoln, including biographies, anecdotes, timelines, quotes, primary documents, images, and more.

Freedman, R. *Lincoln: A Photobiography*. New York: Clarion Books, 1987.

Hakim, J. Book Six: "War, Terrible War." *A History of US*. New York: Oxford University Press, 1999.

Hakim, J. Book Eleven: "Sourcebook and Index: Documents that Shaped the American Nation." *A History of US*. New York: Oxford University Press, 1999.

Modern History Sourcebook
http://www.fordham.edu/halsall/mod/modsbook.htm

For Teachers

Miller, W. L. *Lincoln's Virtues: An Ethical Biography*. New York: Knopf, 2002.

Beran, M. K. "Lincoln, *MacBeth*, and the Moral Imagination." *Humanitas*, Volume XI, No.2, 1998.

Abraham Lincoln:
The Gettysburg Address,
November 19, 1863

President Lincoln gave this speech at a ceremony at Gettysburg, to dedicate the battlefield to the soldiers who had died there. He spoke for two minutes after Edward Everett, a renowned orator from Massachusetts, had spoken for two hours. The cameraman intended to photograph the President, but he had not even finished setting up his camera by the time the speech was over.

Fourscore and seven years ago our fathers brought forth on this continent a new nation, conceived in Liberty, and dedicated to the proposition that all men are created equal.

Now we are engaged in a great Civil War, testing whether that nation, or any nation so conceived and so dedicated, can long endure. We are met on a great battlefield of that war. We have come to dedicate a portion of that field, as final resting place for those who here gave their lives that that nation might live. It is altogether fitting and proper that we should do this.

But, in a larger sense, we cannot dedicate—we cannot consecrate—we cannot hallow this ground. The brave men, living and dead, who struggled here, have consecrated it, far above our poor power to add or detract. The world will little note, nor long remember, what we say here, but it can never forget what they did here. It is for us the living, rather, to be dedicated here to the unfinished work which they who fought here have thus far so nobly advanced. It is rather for us to be here dedicated to the great task remaining before us—that from these honored dead we take increased devotion to that cause for which they gave the last full measure of devotion—that we here highly resolve that these dead shall not have died in vain—that this nation, under God, shall have a new birth of freedom—and that government of the people, by the people, for the people, shall not perish from the earth.

Abraham Lincoln:
"A House Divided"
Address to the Illinois Republican Convention (1858)

Mr. President and Gentlemen of the Convention:

If we could first know where we are and whither we are tending, we could better judge what to do and how to do it. We are now far into the fifth year since a policy was initiated with the avowed object and confident promise of putting an end to slavery agitation. Under the operation of that policy, that agitation has not only not ceased but has constantly augmented. In my opinion, it will not cease until a crisis shall have been reached and passed. "A house divided against itself cannot stand." I believe this government cannot endure, permanently, half slave and half free. I do not expect the Union to be dissolved; I do not expect the house to fall; but I do expect it will cease to be divided. It will become all one thing, or all the other. Either the opponents of slavery will arrest the further spread of it and place it where the public mind shall rest in the belief that it is in the course of ultimate extinction, or its advocates will push it forward till it shall become alike lawful in all the states, old as well as new, North as well as South.

Have we no tendency to the latter condition?

Let anyone who doubts carefully contemplate that now almost complete legal combination—piece of machinery, so to speak—compounded of the Nebraska doctrine and the Dred Scott decision. Let him consider, not only what work the machinery is adapted to do, and how well adapted, but also let him study the history of its construction and trace, if he can, or rather fail, if he can, to trace the evidences of design and concert of action among its chief architects, from the beginning.

The new year of 1854 found slavery excluded from more than half the states by state constitutions and from most of the national territory by congressional prohibition. Four days later commenced the struggle which ended in repealing that congressional prohibition. This opened all the national territory to slavery and was the first point gained.

But, so far, Congress only had acted; and an endorsement by the people, real or apparent, was indispensable to save the point already gained and give chance for more.

This necessity had not been overlooked, but had been provided for, as well as might be, in the notable argument of "squatter sovereignty," otherwise called "sacred right of self-government," which latter phrase, though expressive of the only rightful basis of any government, was so perverted in this attempted use of it as to amount to just this: That if any one man choose to enslave another, no third man shall be allowed to object. That argument was incorporated into the Nebraska Bill itself, in the language which follows:

> It being the true intent and meaning of this act not to legislate slavery into an territory or state, nor to exclude it therefrom, but to leave the people there-of perfectly free to form and regulate their domestic institutions in their own way, subject only to the Constitution of the United States.

Then opened the roar of loose declamation in favor of "squatter sovereignty" and "sacred right of self-government." "But," said opposition members, "let us amend the bill so as to expressly declare that the people of the territory may exclude slavery." "Not we," said the friends of the measure; and down they voted the amendment.

While the Nebraska Bill was passing through Congress, a law case, involving the question of a Negro's freedom, by reason of his owner having voluntarily taken him first into a free state and then into a territory covered by the congressional prohibition, and held him as a slave for a long time in each, was passing through the United States Circuit Court for the district of Missouri; and both Nebraska Bill and lawsuit were brought to a decision in the same month of May 1854. The Negro's name was Dred Scott, which name now designates the decision finally made in the case. Before the next presidential election, the law case came to, and was argued in, the Supreme Court of the United States; but the decision of it was deferred until after the election. Still, before the election, Senator Trumbull, on the floor of the Senate, requested the leading advocate of the Nebraska Bill to state his opinion whether the people of a territory can constitutionally exclude slavery from their limits; and the latter answers: "That is a question for the Supreme Court."

The election came. Mr. Buchanan was elected, and the endorsement, such as it was, secured. That was the second point gained. The endorsement, however, fell short of a clear popular majority by nearly 400,000 votes, and so, perhaps, was not overwhelmingly reliable and satisfactory. The outgoing President, in his last annual message, as impressively as possible echoed back upon the people the weight and authority of the endorsement. The Supreme Court met again, did not announce their decision, but ordered a reargument.

The presidential inauguration came, and still no decision of the Court; but the incoming President, in his inaugural address, fervently exhorted the people to abide by the forthcoming decision, whatever it might be. Then, in a few days, came the decision.

The reputed author of the Nebraska Bill finds an early occasion to make a speech at this capital endorsing the Dred Scott decision, and vehemently denouncing all opposition to it. The new President, too, seizes the early occasion of the Silliman letter to endorse and strongly construe that decision, and to express his astonishment that any different view had ever been entertained!

At length a squabble springs up between the President and the author of the Nebraska Bill, on the mere question of fact, whether the Lecompton constitution was or was not in any just sense made by the people of Kansas; and in that quarrel the latter declares that all he wants is a fair vote for the people, and that he cares not whether slavery be voted down or voted up. I do not understand his declaration, that he cares not whether slavery be voted down or voted up, to be intended by him other than as an apt definition of the policy he would impress upon the public mind—the principle for which he declares he has suffered so much and is ready to suffer to the end. And well may he cling to that principle! If he has any parental feeling, well may he cling to it. That principle is the only shred left of his original Nebraska doctrine.

Under the Dred Scott decision, "squatter sovereignty" squatted out of existence, tumbled down like temporary scaffolding; like the mold at the foundry, served through one blast and fell back into loose sand; helped to carry an election and then was kicked to the winds. His late joint struggle with the Republicans against the Lecompton constitution involves nothing of the original Nebraska doctrine. That struggle was made on a point—the right of a people to make their own constitution—upon which he and the Republicans have never differed.

The several points of the Dred Scott decision, in connection with Senator Douglas' "care not" policy, constitute the piece of machinery in its present state of advancement. This was the third point gained. The working points of that machinery are:

First, that no Negro slave, imported as such from Africa, and no descendant of such slave can ever be a citizen of any state in the sense of that term as used in the Constitution of the United States. This point is made in order to deprive the Negro, in every possible event, of the benefit of that provision of the United States Constitution which declares that "the citizens of each state shall be entitled to all the privileges and immunities of citizens in the several states."

Second, that, "subject to the Constitution of the United States," neither Congress nor a territorial legislature can exclude slavery from any United States territory. This point is made in order that individual men may fill up the territories with slaves, without danger of losing them as property, and thus enhance the chances of permanency to the institution through all the future.

Third, that whether the holding a Negro in actual slavery in a free state makes him free, as against the holder, the United States courts will not decide, but will leave to be decided by the courts of any slave state the Negro may be forced into by the master. This point is made, not to be pressed immediately but, if acquiesced in for awhile, and apparently endorsed by the people at an election, then to sustain the logical conclusion that what Dred Scott's master might lawfully do with Dred Scott in the free state of Illinois, every other master may lawfully do with any other one, or 1,000 slaves, in Illinois or in any other free state.

Auxiliary to all this, and working hand in hand with it, the Nebraska doctrine, or what is left of it, is to educate and mold public opinion, at least Northern public opinion, not to care whether slavery is voted down or voted up. This shows exactly where we now are; and partially, also, whither we are tending.

It will throw additional light on the latter to go back and run the mind over the string of historical facts already stated. Several things will now appear less dark and mysterious than they did when they were transpiring. The people were to be left "perfectly free," "subject only to the Constitution." What the Constitution had to do with it, outsiders could not then see. Plainly enough, now, it was an exactly fitted niche for the Dred Scott decision to afterward come in and declare the perfect freedom of the people to be just no freedom at all.

Why was the amendment expressly declaring the right of the people voted down? Plainly enough, now, the adoption of it would have spoiled the niche for the Dred Scott decision. Why was the Court decision held up? Why even a senator's individual opinion withheld till after the presidential election? Plainly enough, now, the speaking out then would have damaged the "perfectly free" argument upon which the election was to be carried. Why the outgoing President's felicitation on the endorsement? Why the delay of a reargument? Why the incoming President's advance exhortation in favor of the decision? These things look like the cautious patting and petting of a spirited horse preparatory to mounting him when it is dreaded that he may give the rider a fall. And why the hasty after-endorsement of the decision by the President and others?

We cannot absolutely know that all these exact adaptations are the result of preconcert. But when we see a lot of framed timbers, different portions of which we know have been gotten out at different times and places and by different workmen—Stephen, Franklin, Roger, and James, for instance—and when we see these timbers joined together and see they exactly make the frame of a house or a mill, all the tenons and mortises exactly fitting, and all the lengths and proportions of the different pieces exactly adapted to their respective places, and not a piece too many or too few, not omitting even scaffolding, or, if a single piece be lacking, we see the place in the frame exactly fitted and prepared yet to bring such piece in—in such a case, we find it impossible not to believe that Stephen and Franklin and Roger and James all understood one another from the beginning, and all worked upon a common plan or draft drawn up before the first blow was struck.

Reprinted from Annals of America. © 1968, 1976 Encyclopedia Brittanica, Inc.

http://www.pbs.org/wgbh/aia/part4/4h2934t.html

Abraham Lincoln:
The Emancipation Proclamation (1863)

By the President of the United States of America:

A PROCLAMATION

Whereas on the 22nd day of September, A.D. 1862, a proclamation was issued by the President of the United States, containing, among other things, the following, to wit:

"That on the 1st day of January, A.D. 1863, all persons held as slaves within any State or designated part of a State the people whereof shall then be in rebellion against the United States shall be then, thenceforward, and forever free; and the executive government of the United States, including the military and naval authority thereof, will recognize and maintain the freedom of such persons and will do no act or acts to repress such persons, or any of them, in any efforts they may make for their actual freedom.

"That the executive will on the 1st day of January aforesaid, by proclamation, designate the States and parts of States, if any, in which the people thereof, respectively, shall then be in rebellion against the United States; and the fact that any State or the people thereof shall on that day be in good faith represented in the Congress of the United States by members chosen thereto at elections wherein a majority of the qualified voters of such States shall have participated shall, in the absence of strong countervailing testimony, be deemed conclusive evidence that such State and the people thereof are not then in rebellion against the United States."

Now, therefore, I, Abraham Lincoln, President of the United States, by virtue of the power in me vested as Commander-In-Chief of the Army and Navy of the United States in time of actual armed rebellion against the authority and government of the United States, and as a fit and necessary war measure for supressing said rebellion, do, on this 1st day of January, A.D. 1863, and in accordance with my purpose so to do, publicly proclaimed for the full period of one hundred days from the first day above mentioned, order and designate as the States and parts of States wherein the people thereof, respectively, are this day in rebellion against the United States the following, to wit:

Arkansas, Texas, Louisiana (except the parishes of St. Bernard, Palquemines, Jefferson, St. John, St. Charles, St. James, Ascension, Assumption, Terrebone, Lafourche, St. Mary, St. Martin, and Orleans, including the city of New Orleans), Mississippi, Alabama, Florida, Georgia, South Carolina, North Carolina, and Virginia (except the forty-eight counties designated as West Virginia, and also the counties of Berkeley, Accomac, Morthhampton, Elizabeth City, York, Princess Anne, and Norfolk, including the cities of Norfolk and Portsmouth), and which excepted parts are for the present left precisely as if this proclamation were not issued.

And by virtue of the power and for the purpose aforesaid, I do order and declare that all persons held as slaves within said designated States and parts of States are, and henceforward shall be, free; and that the Executive Government of the United States, including the military and naval authorities thereof, will recognize and maintain the freedom of said persons.

And I hereby enjoin upon the people so declared to be free to abstain from all violence, unless in necessary self-defence; and I recommend to them that, in all case when allowed, they labor faithfully for reasonable wages.

And I further declare and make known that such persons of suitable condition will be received into the armed service of the United States to garrison forts, positions, stations, and other places, and to man vessels of all sorts in said service.

And upon this act, sincerely believed to be an act of justice, warranted by the Constitution upon military necessity, I invoke the considerate judgment of mankind and the gracious favor of Almighty God.

http://odur.let.rug.nl/~usa/P/al16/writings/emancip.htm

Abraham Lincoln:
Second Inaugural Address (March 4, 1865)

Fellow Countrymen:

At this second appearing to take the oath of the presidential office, there is less occasion for an extended address than there was at the first. Then a statement, somewhat in detail, of a course to be pursued, seemed fitting and proper. Now, at the expiration of four years, during which public declarations have been constantly called forth on every point and phase of the great contest which still absorbs the attention, and engrosses the energies [sic] of the nation, little that is new could be presented. The progress of our arms, upon which all else chiefly depends, is as well known to the public as to myself; and it is, I trust, reasonably satisfactory and encouraging to all. With high hope for the future, no prediction in regard to it so ventured.

On the occasion corresponding to this four years ago, all thoughts were anxiously directed to an impending civil-war. All dreaded it—all sought to avert it. While the inaugural address was being delivered from this place, devoted altogether to saving the Union without war, insurgent agents were in the city seeking to destroy it without war—seeking to dissolve the Union, and divide effects, by negotiation. Both parties deprecated war; but one of them would make war rather than let the nation survive; and others would accept war rather than let it perish. And the war came.

One eighth of the whole population were colored slaves, not distributed generally over the Union, but localized in the Southern part of it. These slaves constituted a peculiar and powerful interest. All knew that this interest was somehow, the cause of the war. To strengthen, perpetuate, and extend this interest was the object for which the insurgents would rend the Union, even by war; while the government claimed no right to do more than to restrict the territorial enlargement of it. Neither party expected for the war, the magnitude, or the duration, which it has already attained. Neither anticipated that the cause of the conflict might cease with, or even before, the conflict itself should cease. Each looked for an easier triumph, and a result less fundamental and astounding. Both read the same Bible, and pray to the same God; and each invokes His aid against the other. It may seem strange that any men should dare ask a just God's assistance in wringing their bread from the sweat of other men's faces; but let us judge not that we will be not judged.[1] The prayers of both could not be answered; that of neither has been answered fully. The Almighty has His own purposes. Woe unto the world because of offenses! for it must needs be that offenses come; but woe to that man by whom the offense cometh![2] If we shall suppose that American Slavery is one of those offenses which, in the providence of God, must needs come, but which, having continued through His appointed time, He now wills to remove, and that He gives to both North and South, this terrible war, as the woe due to those by whom the offense came, shall we discern therein any departure from those divine attributes which the believers in a Living God always ascribe to Him? Fondly do we hope—fervently do we pray—that this mighty scourge of war may speedily pass away. Yet, if God wills that it continue, until all the wealth piled by the bond-man's two hundred and fifty years of unrequited toil shall be sunk, and until every drop of blood drawn with the lash, shall be paid by another drawn with the sword, as was said three thousand years ago, so still it must be said the judgments of the Lord, are true and righteous altogether.[3]

With malice toward none; with charity for all; with firmness in the right, as God gives us to see the right, let us strive on to finish the work we are in, to bind up the nation's wounds; to care for him who shall have borne the battle, and for his widow, and his orphan—to do all which may achieve and cherish a just, and a lasting peace, among ourselves, and with all nations.

---

[1]Matthew 7:1.
[2]Matthew 18:7.
[3]Psalms 19:9.

http://www.fordham.edu/halsall/mod/1865lincoln-aug2.html

I had crossed the line. I was free; but there was no one to welcome me to the land of freedom. I was a stranger in a strange land.

—Harriet Tubman

COMPASSION

COMPASSION: The desire to alleviate the sufferings of others.

Deficiency: Apathy	COMPASSION	Excess: Sentimentalism

Students will examine the life of Harriet Tubman during their studies of the events leading up to the Civil War. Even after she escaped from slavery and was living relatively comfortably in the North, she willingly put her own life in danger so that she could lead other slaves to freedom. Her compassion for her fellow human beings is a valuable example for students.

BACKGROUND

The following biographical information serves as a short description of the life of Harriet Tubman. It is suggested that students read a biography such as *Harriet Tubman: Conductor on the Underground Railroad* by Ann Petry before beginning this lesson.

Harriet Tubman was a black American woman who rescued hundreds of slaves from the South by helping them escape to freedom. She was born a slave in Bucktown, Md., prior to the Civil War. When she was a young girl her father taught her valuable information about the woods, such as how to tread softly without being heard, which was knowledge she would later use during her perilous rescue missions. Although her family was near her when she was young, she was subject to frequent whippings and other cruelties from her owners. She was once forced to wade through cold water when she had bronchitis and the measles, and she almost died from the illness that resulted. When she finally recovered, she had a deep, husky voice that she would never be rid of.

From a young age, Tubman recognized the importance of compassion, and she displayed this virtue in her own life. At the age of thirteen, she refused to help an overseer chase a fellow slave who was running away from him. The supervisor threw a two-pound lead weight at Tubman's head and fractured her skull. She suffered blackouts for the rest of her life.

Tubman escaped to Philadelphia through the Underground Railroad in 1849, which was a system that helped slaves flee to free states or to Canada. The Railroad consisted of a series of hiding places, such as houses or barns (called "stations") where slaves were led by "conductors" to hide until they could get to a free state. Tubman resolved to help other slaves escape as she had, and she became the most famous "conductor" of the Underground Railroad.

Risking her own life, Tubman made her first trip back to Maryland after Congress passed the Fugitive Slave Law of 1850, a law that mandated the return to his or her owner of any runaway slave who fled to the North. She made eighteen trips during the 1850s and helped to free more than 3,000 slaves. Naturally, her willingness to help slaves escape enraged slave owners and slave-catchers, and at one time the rewards for her capture totaled $40,000. Despite the overwhelming odds against her, Tubman was never caught, and she boasted that she never lost a passenger on any of the rescue trips. Her ingenuity and her knowledge about the woods that she had acquired as a child saved the rescue missions from several close calls with slave-catchers. Travelers on the railroad walked all night in the cold, and Tubman would sometimes whistle or sing in the dark to let her passengers know where she was. Some of these songs, such as "Follow the Drinking Gourd," still survive today. Tubman earned the nickname "Moses" because she led so many slaves to freedom.

Tubman also served the Union army during the Civil War. She worked as a nurse, scout, and spy in South Carolina, all without pay. After the war she raised money for black schools in Auburn, Ala. In 1908 she started a home for elderly and needy blacks.

Harriet Tubman is an example of a person with the compassion and courage that helped to make a difference in the lives of others and the history of our nation.

Awareness

Write the definition of *compassion* from the beginning of the lesson on the board. Ask students what compassion means to them. Does showing people compassion mean giving them whatever they want? How did Tubman show compassion for others? What decisions did she make? What risks did she take? Why?

Understanding

Following the introduction to Harriet Tubman, ask students to read the story of Moses from the *Book of Exodus*. Draw attention to 12:29-14:30, in which Moses leads the Israelites out of Egypt. Comparing the lives of Moses and Tubman will help students to understand the significance of her nickname and how it reflects her character.

- **How did Moses and Tubman show compassion for enslaved peoples?**
- **Was Tubman worthy of her nickname? What makes you think so?**

Neither Tubman nor Moses had very difficult lives when they made choices to help those who were suffering around them. (Tubman had escaped to a free state and Moses had been raised as the son of the Pharaoh's daughter.) Does that take away from their accomplishments? Why should we show compassion for others, even when their problems do not appear to concern us?

Action

A compassion challenge

Encourage students to reach out and practice acts of compassion when they see people in need at home and at school. Practicing compassion does not have to involve large-scale acts such as the ones Harriet Tubman practiced. She simply recognized a problem and set out to alleviate it. Discuss ways that students can identify needs that can be met with acts of compassion, such as:

- helping a classmate who is having difficulty understanding an assignment,
- helping an overwhelmed parent with household chores, or
- comforting a friend who is experiencing stress over troubles in a relationship.

Challenge students to engage in compassionate acts over a one-week period.

Community service | Following Tubman's example, have the class brainstorm a plan for reaching out to the community at large. Some suggestions are to visit the elderly in a local rest home, to volunteer to tutor small children, or to hold a fundraiser to raise money for a cancer society. Have students create an action plan to put their ideas into practice, then have them implement their plan.

Reflection

A tribute to Tubman

Ask students to write a speech or letter of gratitude offering tribute to Harriet Tubman. Encourage them to highlight some of her choices and deeds that have left an imprint on our collective memory.

On the compassion challenge

Encourage students to keep a journal to reflect on the acts of compassion that they practiced throughout the week. Have students answer the following questions:

- What was the need or situation to which you responded?
- Did it ever occur to you to help this person in need before?
- What were the outcomes of the acts for the recipients?
- How did the experience feel to you?
- In addition to Harriet Tubman, is there another person who may have served as an example for what you should do? In what ways does that individual display compassion?

On the service project

Lead an in-class debriefing session upon completion of the community service project. Was the project worthwhile? What made it so? Does any member of the class have any anecdotes/experiences to share?

Bibliography

For Students and Teachers

Tubman image from: www.psouth.net/~debbyp/women.html

Exodus. *The Holy Bible*. Revised Standard Version. New York: Penguin Books, 1962.

http://quest.arc.nasa.gov/ltc/special/mlk/gourd2.html

Hakim, J. "War, Terrible War." *A History of US*. New York: Oxford University Press, 1999.

Petry, A. *Harriet Tubman: Conductor on the Underground Railroad*. New York: Harper Trophy, 1996.

Schraff, A. E. *Harriet Tubman: Moses of the Underground Railroad*. Berkeley Heights: Enslow Publishers, 2001.

Harriet Tubman, shown here on the far left, posing with a group of slaves that she led through the Underground Railroad.

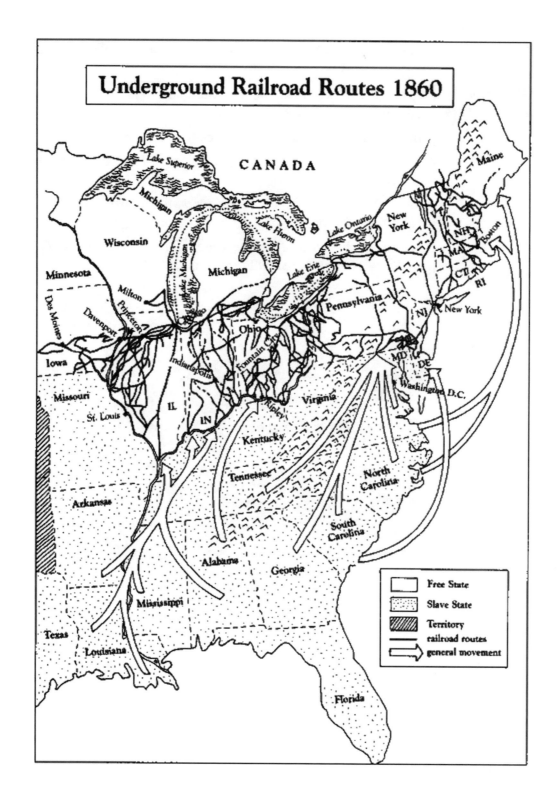

http://education.ucdavis.edu/NEW/STC/lesson/socstud/railroad/Map.htm

Follow the Drinking Gourd

Harriet Tubman and other conductors of the Underground Railroad used this coded song to give slaves directions to the free states. The "drinking gourd" is the Big Dipper. "When the sun comes back" tells the slaves that they should leave in the winter, when the sun begins to climb higher in the sky. Other landmarks direct them to the Ohio River in the last verse, where they would cross to the north bank and meet another guide from the Underground Railroad.

Follow the drinking gourd!
Follow the drinking gourd.
For the old man is awaiting for to carry you
to freedom
If you follow the drinking gourd.

When the sun comes back and the first quail calls,
Follow the drinking gourd,
For the old man is awaiting for to carry you
to freedom
If you follow the drinking gourd.

The riverbank makes a very good road,
The dead trees will show you the way,
Left foot, peg foot traveling on,
Following the drinking gourd.

The river ends between two hills,
Follow the drinking gourd,
There's another river on the other side,
Follow the drinking gourd.

Where the great big river meets the little river,
Follow the drinking gourd,
The old man is awaiting for to carry you to freedom
If you follow the drinking gourd.

Lyrics from http://quest.arc.nasa.gov/ltc/special/mlk/gourd2.html

The Exodus

This excerpt from the book of Exodus in the Bible relates how Moses guided the Israelites out of Egypt, ending with the parting of the Red Sea.

Chapter 12

29 At midnight the LORD smote all the first-born in the land of Egypt, from the first-born of Pharaoh who sat on his throne to the first-born of the captive who was in the dungeon, and all the first-born of the cattle. 30 And Pharaoh rose up in the night, he, and all his servants, and all the Egyptians; and there was a great cry in Egypt, for there was not a house where one was not dead. 31 And he summoned Moses and Aaron by night, and said, "Rise up, go forth from among my people, both you and the people of Israel; and go, serve the LORD, as you have said. 32 Take your flocks and your herds, as you have said, and be gone; and bless me also!"

33 And the Egyptians were urgent with the people, to send them out of the land in haste; for they said, "We are all dead men." 34 So the people took their dough before it was leavened, their kneading bowls being bound up in their mantles on their shoulders. 35 The people of Israel had also done as Moses told them, for they had asked of the Egyptians jewelry of silver and of gold, and clothing; 36 and the LORD had given the people favor in the sight of the Egyptians, so that they let them have what they asked. Thus they despoiled the Egyptians.

37 And the people of Israel journeyed from Rameses to Succoth, about six hundred thousand men on foot, besides women and children. 38 A mixed multitude also went up with them, and very many cattle, both flocks and herds. 39 And they baked unleavened cakes of the dough which they had brought out of Egypt, for it was not leavened, because they were thrust out of Egypt and could not tarry, neither had they prepared for themselves any provisions.

40 The time that the people of Israel dwelt in Egypt was four hundred and thirty years. 41 And at the end of four hundred and thirty years, on that very day, all the hosts of the LORD went out from the land of Egypt. 42 It was a night of watching by the LORD, to bring them out of the land of Egypt; so this same night is a night of watching kept to the LORD by all the people of Israel throughout their generations.

43 And the LORD said to Moses and Aaron, "This is the ordinance of the passover: no foreigner shall eat of it; 44 but every slave that is bought for money may eat of it after you have circumcised him. 45 No sojourner or hired servant may eat of it. 46 In one house shall it be eaten; you shall not carry forth any of the flesh outside the house; and you shall not break a bone of it. 47 All the congregation of Israel shall keep it. 48 And when a stranger shall sojourn with you and would keep the passover to the LORD, let all his males be circumcised, then he may come near and keep it; he shall be as a native of the land. But no uncircumcised person shall eat of it. 49 There shall be one law for the native and for the stranger who sojourns among you."

50 Thus did all the people of Israel; as the LORD commanded Moses and Aaron, so they did. 51 And on that very day the LORD brought the people of Israel out of the land of Egypt by their hosts.

Chapter 13

1 The LORD said to Moses, 2 "Consecrate to me all the first-born; whatever is the first to open the womb among the people of Israel, both of man and of beast, is mine."

3 And Moses said to the people, "Remember this day, in which you came out from Egypt, out of the house of bondage, for by strength of hand the LORD brought you out from this place; no leavened bread shall be eaten. 4 This day you are to go forth, in the month of Abib. 5 And when the LORD brings you into the land of the Canaanites, the Hittites, the Amorites, the Hivites, and the Jebusites, which he swore to your fathers to give you, a land flowing with milk and honey, you shall keep this service in this month. 6 Seven days you shall eat unleavened bread, and on the seventh day there shall be a feast to the LORD. 7 Unleavened bread shall be eaten for seven days; no leavened bread shall be seen with you, and no leaven shall be seen with you in all your territory. 8 And you shall tell your son on that day, 'It is because of what the LORD did for me when I came out of Egypt.' 9 And it shall be to you as a sign on your hand and as a memorial between your eyes, that the law of the LORD may be in your mouth; for with a strong hand the LORD has brought you out of Egypt. 10 You shall therefore keep this ordinance at its appointed time from year to year.

11 "And when the LORD brings you into the land of the Canaanites, as he swore to you and your fathers, and shall give it to you, 12 you shall set

apart to the LORD all that first opens the womb. All the firstlings of your cattle that are males shall be the LORD's. 13 Every firstling of an ass you shall redeem with a lamb, or if you will not redeem it you shall break its neck. Every first-born of man among your sons you shall redeem. 14 And when in time to come your son asks you, 'What does this mean?' you shall say to him, 'By strength of hand the LORD brought us out of Egypt, from the house of bondage. 15 For when Pharaoh stubbornly refused to let us go, the LORD slew all the first-born in the land of Egypt, both the first-born of man and the first-born of cattle. Therefore I sacrifice to the LORD all the males that first open the womb; but all the first-born of my sons I redeem.' 16 It shall be as a mark on your hand or frontlets between your eyes; for by a strong hand the LORD brought us out of Egypt."

17 When Pharaoh let the people go, God did not lead them by way of the land of the Philistines, although that was near; for God said, "Lest the people repent when they see war, and return to Egypt." 18 But God led the people round by the way of the wilderness toward the Red Sea. And the people of Israel went up out of the land of Egypt equipped for battle. 19 And Moses took the bones of Joseph with him; for Joseph had solemnly sworn the people of Israel, saying, "God will visit you; then you must carry my bones with you from here." 20 And they moved on from Succoth, and encamped at Etham, on the edge of the wilderness. 21 And the LORD went before them by day in a pillar of cloud to lead them along the way, and by night in a pillar of fire to give them light, that they might travel by day and by night; 22 the pillar of cloud by day and the pillar of fire by night did not depart from before the people.

Chapter 14

1 Then the LORD said to Moses, 2 "Tell the people of Israel to turn back and encamp in front of Pi-ha-hiroth, between Migdol and the sea, in front of Baal-zephon; you shall encamp over against it, by the sea. 3 For Pharaoh will say of the people of Israel, 'They are entangled in the land; the wilderness has shut them in.' 4 And I will harden Pharaoh's heart, and he will pursue them and I will get glory over Pharaoh and all his host; and the Egyptians shall know that I am the LORD." And they did so.

5 When the king of Egypt was told that the people had fled, the mind of Pharaoh and his servants was changed toward the people, and they said,

"What is this we have done, that we have let Israel go from serving us?" 6 So he made ready his chariot and took his army with him, 7 and took six hundred picked chariots and all the other chariots of Egypt with officers over all of them. 8 And the LORD hardened the heart of Pharaoh king of Egypt and he pursued the people of Israel as they went forth defiantly. 9 The Egyptians pursued them, all Pharaoh's horses and chariots and his horsemen and his army, and overtook them encamped at the sea, by Pi-ha-hiroth, in front of Baal-zephon.

10 When Pharaoh drew near, the people of Israel lifted up their eyes, and behold, the Egyptians were marching after them; and they were in great fear. And the people of Israel cried out to the LORD; 11 and they said to Moses, "Is it because there are no graves in Egypt that you have taken us away to die in the wilderness? What have you done to us, in bringing us out of Egypt? 12 Is not this what we said to you in Egypt, 'Let us alone and let us serve the Egyptians'? For it would have been better for us to serve the Egyptians than to die in the wilderness." 13 And Moses said to the people, "Fear not, stand firm, and see the salvation of the LORD, which he will work for you today; for the Egyptians whom you see today, you shall never see again. 14 The LORD will fight for you, and you have only to be still." 15 The LORD said to Moses, "Why do you cry to me? Tell the people of Israel to go forward. 16 Lift up your rod, and stretch out your hand over the sea and divide it, that the people of Israel may go on dry ground through the sea. 17 And I will harden the hearts of the Egyptians so that they shall go in after them, and I will get glory over Pharaoh and all his host, his chariots, and his horsemen. 18 And the Egyptians shall know that I am the LORD, when I have gotten glory over Pharaoh, his chariots, and his horsemen."

19 Then the angel of God who went before the host of Israel moved and went behind them; and the pillar of cloud moved from before them and stood behind them, 20 coming between the host of Egypt and the host of Israel. And there was the cloud and the darkness; and the night passed without one coming near the other all night.

21 Then Moses stretched out his hand over the sea; and the LORD drove the sea back by a strong east wind all night, and made the sea dry land, and the waters were divided. 22 And the people of Israel went into the midst of the sea on dry ground, the waters being a wall to them on their right hand and on their left. 23 The Egyptians pursued, and went in after them into the

midst of the sea, all Pharaoh's horses, his chariots, and his horsemen. 24 And in the morning watch the LORD in the pillar of fire and of cloud looked down upon the host of the Egyptians, and discomfited the host of the Egyptians, 25 clogging their chariot wheels so that they drove heavily; and the Egyptians said, "Let us flee from before Israel; for the LORD fights for them against the Egyptians."

26 Then the LORD said to Moses, "Stretch out your hand over the sea, that the water may come back upon the Egyptians, upon their chariots, and upon their horsemen." 27 So Moses stretched forth his hand over the sea, and the sea returned to its wonted flow when the morning appeared; and the Egyptians fled into it, and the LORD routed the Egyptians in the midst of the sea. 28 The waters returned and covered the chariots and the horsemen and all the host of Pharaoh that had followed them into the sea; not so much as one of them remained. 29 But the people of Israel walked on dry ground through the sea, the waters being a wall to them on their right hand and on their left.

30 Thus the LORD saved Israel that day from the hand of the Egyptians; and Israel saw the Egyptians dead upon the seashore. 31 And Israel saw the great work which the LORD did against the Egyptians, and the people feared the LORD; and they believed in the LORD and in his servant Moses.

Source: "Exodus, Revised Standard Version." *Ancient History Sourcebook*.
http://www.fordham.edu/halsall/ancient/exodus-rsv.html

You must never so much as think whether you like it or not, whether it is bearable or not; you must never think of anything except the need and how to meet it.

—Clara Barton

GENEROSITY

GENEROSITY: The willingness to give or share without expecting anything in return; being unselfish.

Deficiency: **Stinginess**	—	**GENEROSITY**	—	Excess: **Wastefulness**

This lesson is intended to prompt thought, discussion, and practice of the virtue of generosity, using the life of Clara Barton as an example. It may be taught in conjunction with an American Civil War unit or a unit on woman leaders.

BACKGROUND

The following short biography highlights Barton's generosity. Teachers are encouraged to assign students to read a biography such as *Clara Barton: Healing the Wounds* by C. E. Dubowski to learn more about Barton's life and accomplishments.

Clarissa Harlowe Barton was born on December 25, 1821, in North Oxford, Mass. She was the youngest of five children, and her two brothers and two sisters assumed much of the responsibility for her education. With their help, Barton received a vast and diverse schooling. By the time she started school at age four, Clara could already spell three-syllable words. As she grew older, she studied subjects such as philosophy, chemistry, and Latin, but found school to be quite easy. Clara's only handicap was her extreme shyness.

When Clara was 11 years old, one of her brothers, David, was severely injured in a fall from the barn roof. The only person he wanted to nurse him back to health was his younger sister Clara. Her parents had to acquire permission for her to stay at home and miss school, but it proved to be a wise decision. Even at a young age Clara showed signs of being a gentle and caring nurse. She was able to use her nursing skills once again when a smallpox epidemic broke out in her early adolescence. Barton traveled to neighbors' homes to offer what comfort and aid she could.

At 17, Barton became a teacher in Massachusetts's District 9, located in Worcester County. During the next six years, she taught in several schools, before establishing her own school in North Oxford. At the age of 29, after teaching for more than ten years, Barton yearned for a change, so she entered the Liberal Institute in Clinton, N.Y., an advanced school for female teachers.

Barton was working at the U.S. Patent Office in Washington, D.C. when the Civil War broke out. She resigned from her job and gave up her own security to volunteer to help distribute bandages, socks, and other goods to wounded soldiers. Barton took a personal interest in the men she aided. When the Sixth Massachusetts Regiment arrived in Washington, D.C. from the battlefield in 1861 with all of their supplies missing, Barton not only requisitioned replacement supplies for the men, but she also personally cooked for them during their stay in the city. In 1862, Barton was granted permission to deliver supplies directly to the front, which she did without fail for the next two years. Known as the "Angel of the Battlefield" she eventually became the superintendent of the Union nurses. She received permission from President Lincoln to begin a letter-writing campaign after the war and to interview Union men returning from Confederate prison camps in order to try to locate missing soldiers.

By 1869, Barton was exhausted, and she traveled to Europe to rest and recuperate on her doctor's orders. Her rest was interrupted, however, when she learned about the Treaty of Geneva, which provided relief to sick and wounded soldiers. Twelve nations had signed the treaty, but the U.S. was not one of them. Barton promised to do something about this and later became a lobbyist for the Treaty. She also learned about the Red Cross by observing the organization in action while traveling with volunteers in the Franco-Prussian War.

When she returned to the United States in 1873, Barton began her crusade for the Treaty of Geneva and the Red Cross. She moved to Washington, D.C. to lobby for her causes. As a result of her efforts, the United States signed the Treaty of Geneva Agreement in 1882. In addition, the American Red Cross organization was formed in 1881, and Barton served as its first president. Several years later she wrote the American amendment to the Red Cross Constitution, which provided for disaster relief during peace time as well as wartime.

Barton remained president of the Red Cross until 1904. During her tenure, she organized and led relief work for disasters such as famines, floods, pestilence, and earthquakes in the United States and throughout the world. The last operation she personally directed was relief for victims of the Galveston, Texas, flood in 1900. In addition, she served as an emissary of the Red Cross and addressed several international conferences.[1]

Awareness

Discuss the definition of *generosity*. Discuss situations in which students can show generosity in their own lives. Does generosity mean giving someone what he or she asks for? Why or why not?

Understanding

Make a list of the contributions or actions of Clara Barton that display her generosity. Ask students to deduce the effects that her generous actions had on other people.

- **What other character traits or virtues does Barton possess?**
- **What reasons did Barton have for acting unselfishly? Did she expect anything in return?**
- **What characteristics of her life and upbringing might have led her to develop generosity as part of her character?**

Help students to realize that Barton was intrinsically motivated to help other people and lobby for important causes because she wanted to improve the lives of many. She acted unselfishly, without regard for danger to herself or the difficulty of the task before her, and she expected nothing in return. The changes she helped to make have had a lasting impact on the lives of Americans. Ask students to remember the impact that showing generosity and being the recipient of generosity has had on them. Ask students to describe a time when they helped someone else without being asked.

- **Why did you do it?**
- **How did it make that person feel? How did it make you feel?**
- **How did it make you feel when some else showed generosity to you?**

---

[1]Biographical overview adapted from research done by Rachel Sahlman.

ACTION

Worthy causes

Ask each student to research a cause that he or she believes to be important. (Veto causes that may be harmful to others or inappropriate for the age level of the students.) Students should research the cause using at least three different sources, and learn about at least one specific organization that supports the cause they choose (e.g., cause: protecting endangered species; organization: World Wildlife Fund). Then ask students to outline a plan for supporting the organization they choose (e.g., what are three ways they could show support?). Students should use their research to learn how they can actually help the people involved. With parental permission, students may even contact the organization to ask what they can do to help (e.g., for the local soup kitchen they may be able to set tables, cook food, wash dishes, etc.). The plans might then be presented to other classes via a website or presentation that focuses on service.

Community service organizations

Divide students into small groups (2-4 people in each) and ask them to create a mock organization that would benefit people in their community. Students should identify an actual cause or need, then discuss and record a plan for creating their organization. Students must consider funding, location, and availability of resources to make the organization as realistic as possible. Students should outline how their organization will benefit the community and what obstacles they may face. Ask each group to share its idea with another group to receive feedback and constructive criticism. Then ask all groups to present their organization plans. Are there any ideas that the entire class could adopt and actually put into effect?

Community organization support

Challenge students to actually support a school- or community-related organization in whatever way they are able (e.g., volunteer to help with the school play, participate in story hour at the local library). Then allow students to discuss their actions and/or update the class on the status of the organization.

Generosity challenge

Ask students to decide on at least three ways that they can show generosity that day. Develop a class list. Then challenge students to carry out these acts at least three times a day and ask them to record and reflect on their generosity and its effects. Alternatively, have students work with partners to carry out acts of generosity.

Reflection

On the community service organization

Ask students to write a short essay on their experiences creating the mock organization. Students should answer the following questions:

- **Was the project more difficult than you originally thought? Why or why not?**
- **How could you make generosity as important in your life as it was in Barton's?**
- **Based on your experiences with the class organization, do you have a better appreciation for what Barton was able to do? Why?**
- **How can you show generosity daily without creating an entire organization?**

On acts of generosity

Ask students to share some generous acts that they or someone they know has performed. What were the motivations behind their generosity? What was the outcome? Explore issues of generosity with the students by asking the following:

- **When is it easy to be generous? When is it difficult?**
- **Does it matter what is at stake, or what you must endure?**
- **Would it be difficult to give up something you value in order to be generous to someone else?**
- **What did Clara Barton risk or need to endure to be generous?**
- **How can we show generosity every day in the classroom or at home?**
- **What acts of generosity take courage?**
- **Can anyone and everyone be generous? What does it take to show generosity?**

Bibliography

Barton image from: http://www.nahc.org/NAHC/Val/columns/SC10-1.html

For Students and Teachers

Dubowski, C. E. *Clara Barton: Healing the Wounds*. New Jersey: Silver Burdett Press, 1991.

Sonneborn, L. *Clara Barton*. New York: Chelsea House, 1992.

Profiles in caring: Clara Barton
http://www.nahc.org/NAHC/Val/columns/SC10-1.html

Ninety-nine percent of the failures come from people who have the habit of making excuses.

—George Washington Carver

DEDICATION

DEDICATION: The habit of devoting one's time, energy or talent to the service of a person or the pursuit of a worthy purpose.

Deficiency: **Indolence, lack of commitment**	**DEDICATION**	Excess: **Blind devotion, fanaticism**

George Washington Carver, the well-known African-American innovator and educator, lived a life of dedication to others. His virtues are worthy of emulation. Students can see and learn the value of dedication through his example.

BACKGROUND

The following is a brief account of Carver's life. Assign students to read a biography such as *George Washington Carver* by Gene Adair to learn more about Carver's life.

George Washington Carver dedicated himself not just to one person, but to many. He committed himself to improving the economic conditions of black farmers in the South. Carver grew up at a time when blacks were denied rights, ("separate but equal" really meant "separate and *unequal*") and people of the South faced poor economic conditions and widespread poverty. Fortunately for Carver, a mentor recognized his talent in horticulture and he was given opportunities that most black people of his time were not.

Carver was born into slavery in 1864. His father died young and his mother was separated from him and his older brother when they were children. The boys were taken to the Carver farm where George helped with the housework and his brother Jim helped with the outdoor chores. Mr. and Mrs. Carver did their best to educate the boys, but it soon became apparent that George's abilities warranted enrollment in a regular school where he could excel. Unfortunately, George could not attend the local whites-only school, so he moved to Neosho, Missouri, to attend the school for black children. Later, he moved to Kansas to attend high school, and graduated from Iowa State College of Agriculture with degrees in Bacterial Botany and Agriculture. Carver worked very hard to put himself through college and even had to drop out temporarily so he could earn more money. Upon graduating, Carver began teaching at Iowa State. He soon moved to Alabama to join Booker T. Washington at the Tuskegee Agricultural and Normal College, which provided higher education to talented black students. There he would be able to achieve his goal of advancing their economic status.

Carver revolutionized agriculture in the early 1900s. Dedicated to improving economic conditions, he began by introducing farmers to crop rotation, and encouraging them to plant crops that would rejuvenate the soil, such as peanuts and sweet potatoes. Unfortunately, consumption of these crops was limited and production was not profitable. Carver was determined to find a solution and he used his ingenuity to create new uses for peanuts and sweet potatoes. From these crops he created many products, including plastics, shampoo, peanut butter, paper and ink. During his lifetime Carver created hundreds of new products.

At Tuskegee, Carver was deeply involved in education and research and directed most of the agricultural department. Carver dedicated himself to teaching and sharing his insights with others. He was passionate about the subjects he taught and tirelessly worked to improve economic conditions for black farmers.

Awareness

Ask students to define *dedication* in their own words, then present the definition above.

- **What is the difference between being dedicated to something, dedicated to someone, or dedicated to some activity? What does each type of dedication entail?**
- **When is it beneficial to be dedicated? What is the difference between dedication and fanaticism and blind devotion? (Ask students to provide examples/scenarios and explain who in them benefits or who is harmed.)**
- **When is it easy to be dedicated? When is it difficult? How can we overcome these difficulties? (Remember that we become dedicated individuals by practicing our dedication, even in demanding situations.)**
- **What are some common ways people show dedication in daily life?**

Understanding

Engage students in a discussion about dedication by asking the following questions:

- **Why do you think George Washington Carver was so dedicated to helping black farmers?**
- **How did others benefit from his work?**
- **What are some of the most striking examples of his dedication?**
- **Ask students to define indolence and list its symptoms. Was Carver free to be indolent if he wanted to be? Why or why not?**
- **What is revealed about Carver through the choices he made?**

Ask students to discuss ways that they show dedication to their own well-being. (Examples may include living drug-free, getting enough sleep, or working diligently to earn good grades.)

Action

Dedication challenge

Arrange opportunities for students to become involved in improving the lives of others, and ask them to dedicate themselves to one project for a set period of time (ideally, at least half of the school year). Examples of activities include reading to kindergarten students, helping fifth graders with schoolwork, visiting with residents at a nursing home, cleaning up the playground after school, etc. Ask colleagues and community members for support in monitoring these activities. Ask students to write a mission statement to explain how they will successfully dedicate themselves, and assign them to keep a weekly journal to record and reflect on the activity and their level of success.

Examples of dedication

Bring in daily newspapers for 2-3 weeks. Allow students time each day to look for articles on people who show dedication. Collect these articles and create a poster or scrapbook. Ask students to continue collecting examples throughout the school year.

Reflection

A speech in honor of Carver

George Washington Carver received many honors in his lifetime and after his death, including the George Washington Carver museum, dedicated at Tuskegee Institute in 1941; the Roosevelt Medal for Outstanding Contribution to Southern Agriculture in 1942; a national monument in Diamond Grove, Mo.; commemorative postage stamps in 1947 and 1998; and a fifty-cent coin in 1951. He was elected to the Hall of Fame for Great Americans in 1977 and inducted posthumously into the National Inventors Hall of Fame in 1990. In 1994, Iowa State University awarded him an honorary Doctor of Humane Letters degree.

Ask students to write a speech that might have been given at an awards ceremony bestowing Carver with one of the honors listed above. The speech should offer evidence of Carver's dedication as the inspiration for granting him the award. As an alternative, students might write the speech from Carver's point of view. Again, the focus of the acceptance speech should be on the dedication entailed in reaching his goals. You may also invite students to create and design an appropriate award to honor Carver in addition to writing the speech.

On Carver's ideals

During his life, George Washington Carver sought "to do the greatest good for the greatest number of his people." Allow students time to brainstorm, then ask them to write an essay explaining 1) how they (individually) can do "the greatest good for the greatest number of people" right now, as middle school students, and 2) how they can offer the greatest good to the greatest number of people in their lifetime.

On the dedication challenge	Ask students to compose an essay in which they focus on an accomplishment that was the fruit of their dedication. Ask students to explain how the desire to achieve that goal arose and to describe the support they received, the outcomes of their dedication, and the difficulties experienced along the way.
Bibliography	Carver image from www.archives.state.al.us/afro/images/carver3re.jpg
For Teachers and Students	Adair, G. *George Washington Carver*. New York: Chelsea House, 1989. A 105-page chapter biography containing many photographs and insights into the life, accomplishments, and struggles of George Washington Carver. *George Washington Carver Biography* http://www.allsands.com/History/People/georgewashingto_yue_gn.htm *The Iowa State University Web Site* http://www.lib.iastate.edu/spcl/gwc/bio.html

Civilization, in the real sense of the term, consists not in the multiplication but in the deliberate and voluntary restriction of wants. This alone promotes real happiness and contentment, and increases the capacity for service.

—Gandhi

SELF-MASTERY

SELF-MASTERY: The habit of moderating one's desires, appetites, or emotions in accordance with reason and a worthy purpose.

Deficiency: **Self-indulgence**	**SELF-MASTERY**	Excess: **Self-neglect**

Students will study the life of Mohandas Gandhi during their studies of imperialism and the British Empire, or as a lesson prior to the study of Martin Luther King. Like St. Augustine, Gandhi lived his youth ruled by his appetites and passions, but he later learned to keep his impulses under control for his own sake and for the good of others. Middle school students are bombarded with temptations, from wasting too much time watching television, surfing the net, or playing video games to overeating, spending beyond their means, and experimenting with drugs and alcohol. Students therefore will benefit from learning about a noble man who faced temptations in his own life.

BACKGROUND

The following background information serves as a short description of the life of Mohandas Gandhi. It is suggested that students read *Gandhi: A Pictoral Biography*, by Gerald Gold, before beginning this lesson.

Remembered as one of the world's greatest teachers, Mohandas Gandhi was born in Porbandar, India in 1869, during the time when India was under British rule. Mohandas's young mother was a model of rigorous self-discipline during his childhood, sometimes fasting several days in a row, which inspired her son's later ascetic lifestyle. According to Hindu customs, Gandhi entered into an arranged marriage at a young age. He was 13; his bride, Kasturba, was 12. Gandhi and Kasturba were barely acquainted with one another when they married, and he found it difficult to control his desire for her. Gandhi's father died when he was 16; Gandhi always believed this tragedy was punishment for his inability to control his lust. He had a family with Kasturba, but he eventually took the vow of *bramacharya*—a life of celibacy—and said late in life that he was truly devoted to his wife only after he had taken the vow.

Gandhi went to London to study law, and then returned to India to practice law for a few years. In 1893, he accepted a contract to do legal work in South Africa. South Africa was run under the apartheid system, which discriminated against and segregated all non-white peoples. While he was there, he was faced with a situation similar to the one Rosa Parks found in the United States more than 50 years later. He was riding in the first-class car of a train when a European sent for an official to remove him to third-class, even though he had a first-class ticket. Gandhi refused to move, so he was thrown off the train, along with all his luggage, and left shivering in the cold night air. The incident made Gandhi resolve to fight against racial injustice. He wrote of his experience, "The hardship to which I was subjected was superficial—only a symptom of the deep disease of colour prejudice. I should try, if possible, to root out the disease and suffer hardships in the process." It was in South Africa that Gandhi adopted the *satyagraha* campaign, named for an Indian word that combines "truth and love" with "firmness." Martin Luther King would later use the same method of "nonviolent resistance" in the American Civil Rights movement. "There is no escape for any of us save through truth and nonviolence," Gandhi wrote. "I know that war is wrong, is an unmitigated evil." Gandhi had the ability to keep his emotions under control. He claimed that he often felt angry at the injustices in India, but chose to act with love rather than with hate.

Gandhi returned to India in 1915 to campaign for Indian independence from Britain. He believed that if Indians were to gain autonomy from the English, then they must no longer accept anything from them. He began to sew his own clothes, using his own spinning wheel to fashion the traditional Hindu garb of a loincloth and a shawl. He also started a large-scale protest against the salt tax and led the famous Salt March 241 miles to the ocean, where he knelt down and picked up a handful of salt at the shore. On the way back, Gandhi was arrested, and his followers attempted to "raid" the British Dharsana saltworks without any aggression towards the owners. Line after line of Indians marched silently up to British guards and allowed themselves to be beaten to the ground without so much as raising an arm against the blows. Images of *satyagraha* in action were broadcast around the world, and this great embarrassment for Britain only helped to fuel sympathy for Gandhi's cause. To his followers Gandhi became known as "Mahatma," or "great soul."

The British arrested Gandhi many times. He frequently exhibited his profound self-mastery on behalf of his people. For instance, he began to campaign for the Untouchables, a class in Hindu society that was at the very bottom of the social ladder and with whom others were forbidden to come in physical contact. "I regard Untouchability as the greatest blot on Hinduism," Gandhi said. "I was hardly yet twelve when this idea had dawned on me. A scavenger named Uka, an Untouchable, used to attend our house for cleaning latrines. Often I would ask my mother why it was wrong to touch him, why I was forbidden to touch him. If I accidentally touched Uka, I was asked to perform the ablutions, and though I naturally obeyed, it was not without smilingly protesting that Untouchability was not sanctioned by religion, that it was impossible that it should be so." Even at his young age, he knew that alienating and labeling others as Untouchables was wrong, and could not have been sanctioned by any Hindu god. In 1932, Gandhi declared that he would fast to the death unless Untouchables were given the same respect as everyone else. Gandhi often fasted several weeks at a time during his campaigning, a few times coming so close to death that the jailers refused to keep him prisoner for fear of their lives if he died. Eventually other Indians began to make compromises and to open their doors to the Untouchables.

India was granted independence on August 15, 1947 and was divided into India and Pakistan. Violence promptly broke out between Hindus and Muslims. Gandhi began another fast to the death as violence continued to engulf Calcutta. The mobs calmed down for fear that Gandhi would die. His hard work to relieve religious tensions was Gandhi's last service to India. On January 30, 1948, he was shot three times in the middle of a prayer meeting and died instantly. The assassin was an orthodox Hindu conspirator who detested Gandhi's preachings of religious toleration.

Awareness	Write the word *self-mastery* on the board. Ask students to brainstorm definitions of this word. What is the difference between self-mastery and self-neglect or masochism? Provide students with examples of each.
Understanding	*Gandhi: A Pictoral Biography*, by Gerald Gold, is a comprehensive source of information about the Mahatma and about the history of India during Gandhi's time, with over a hundred historical photographs. It also contains a bibliography, index, and a map of Gandhi's India.

Ask students to provide examples of how Gandhi showed self-mastery. What were the desires that he attempted to and succeeded in controlling? How did he and others benefit from his ability to contain and redirect his desires?

There is a difference between self-mastery and trying to deny our natural impulses. Ask students why it is harmful to completely deny our natural desires, yet beneficial to keep them under control.

Action

A self-mastery challenge

Gandhi offers us a monumental example of self-mastery with his vow of *brahmacharya* and his ability to fast. He used these techniques because he believed that by mastering his appetite and his emotions, he would become a better person. He also used his self-mastery to inspire others and promote the good of his country.

Every one of us has passions that we need to keep under control in order to prevent them from ruling our lives. These passions can take the form of a particular desire for bodily gratification, such as the unmitigated desire for food or sex. They can take the form of a particular emotion, such as anger or jealousy, or the temptation to do something wrong, such as the desire to lie or steal. Even excessive television watching or video-game playing can distract us from doing what we ought to be doing. In developing the habit of self-mastery we must understand why such passions arise and how we might control them. The way to develop a habit is by practice— continually monitoring our unproductive or destructive tendencies even when temptations seem overwhelming. With practice, it will be easier.

Instruct students to choose a desire or passion that they feel they need to master. Challenge them to set daily goals and to practice self-mastery over this desire for one week.

Reflection

On Gandhi: A Pictoral Biography

After students have finished reading the biography, have them write an essay that answers the following questions:

- **What part of Gandhi's story did you find most surprising or moving?**
- **What motivated Gandhi to exercise self-mastery?**
- **How did his habits help him achieve his goals?**
- **How did his self-mastery help others?**

A letter from prison

Write a letter that Gandhi might have written to his followers while he was in prison. Explain, from his perspective, the importance of self-mastery and the goals he hoped to achieve.

On the self-mastery challenge

Have students write an essay in which they reflect on their personal self-mastery challenge. Students should address the following questions:

- **What was the passion or desire over which you chose to practice self-mastery, and why did you choose it?**
- **What steps did you take to discipline yourself?**
- **Describe the moment(s) during the week when you had the opportunity to practice self-control.**
- **What were your thoughts when your desires felt overwhelming?**
- **What happened to you as a result of your attempts to maintain self-mastery? How did you feel afterwards?**
- **What did you discover about yourself as a person?**
- **In what ways did maintaining the habit of self-mastery become easier or more difficult with time?**
- **What advice do you think Gandhi would give about practice and self-mastery?**

On another historical example of self-mastery

Gandhi once said, "We lift ourselves by our thought, we climb upon our vision of ourselves. If you want to enlarge your life, you must first enlarge your thought of it and of yourself. Hold the ideal of yourself as you long to be, always, everywhere...your ideals of what you long to attain."

Ask students to think of another person from history or contemporary times who has built his or her life around a noble ideal. Identify that ideal and illustrate how the individual demonstrated self-mastery in order to achieve the ideal.

On nonviolent protest	Ask students to write an essay on the power of nonviolent protest. Why do actions speak louder than words sometimes? How did Gandhi's nonverbal methods help him to achieve his goals? How can we apply these methods to modern life?

Bibliography

Gandhi image taken from
www.lucidcafe.com/library/95Oct/mkgandhi.html

For Students and Teachers

The Complete Site on Mahatma Gandhi. www.mkgandhi.org. An excellent resource for teachers and students, this website contains biographies of Gandhi, downloadable full works by Gandhi, quotes, videos, pictures and photographs, timelines, and more. There is also a section especially devoted to students.

Gold, G. *Gandhi: A Pictoral Biography*. New York: Newmarket Press, 1983.

Severance, J. B. *Gandhi, Great Soul*. New York: Clarion Books, 1997.

Recommended Film

Gandhi. Starring Ben Kingsley. Columbia Tristar Studios (1982).

For Teachers

Fischer, L. (ed.). *The Essential Gandhi: An Anthology of His Writings on His Life, Work, and Ideas*. Vintage Books, 2002.

Gandhi. *All Men Are Brothers*. Ed. Krishna Kripalani. New York: Continuum, 2000.

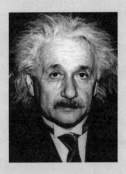

The most important human endeavor is the striving for morality in our actions. Our inner balance and even our very existence depend on it. Only morality in our actions can give beauty and dignity to life.

We have to do the best we can. This is our sacred responsibility.

—Albert Einstein

RESPONSIBILITY

RESPONSIBILITY: The ability to make moral or rational decisions on one's own and to answer for one's behavior; being trustworthy, dependable, and able to distinguish between right and wrong.

RESPONSIBILITY*

*According to Steven S. Tigner, professor of education and philosophy at Boston University, Aristotle views *responsibility* "as a mode of acquiring or exercising virtue (or vice). It's-my-fault certainly lies between it's-not-my-fault and it's-all-my-fault. I-did-it lies between I-didn't-do-it and I-did-it-all. But situations where fault or praise are (un)warranted may be attributable to the presence or exercise of particular relevant virtues or vices. Thus I can be more or less responsible on some occasion because I am cowardly, brave, or reckless; or because I am self-indulgent, temperate, or depressed; or stingy, generous, or ostentatious, and so on." Therefore, according to Aristotle, responsibility itself is not a virtue that lies on a mean; responsibility describes one's commitment to practicing and attaining virtue.

Albert Einstein is considered one of the greatest scientists of the 20th century. Besides being a physicist, Einstein was a humanitarian and ardent antiwar activist, actively involved in struggles around the world to combat racism, anti-Semitism, and nuclear disarmament.

BACKGROUND

Albert Einstein was born on March 14, 1879, in the village of Ulm, Germany to Hermann and Pauline Einstein. His passion for science was ignited with a special birthday gift from his father when he was about five years old: a compass. Trying to discern what made the compass needle move, young Einstein's lifelong sense of wonder regarding the mysteries of the universe, what he later came to refer to as "God's thoughts," took root.

Although it is considered fact that Einstein was not a good student, this is not accurate. Einstein merely lacked the discipline required to master subjects that did not come easily to him, such as languages and history. In math and science, subjects he loved, he was a stellar student. But even his commitment to these subjects weakened under the rigid curriculum and strict formal schooling in Germany. Rebelling against these constraints, he enrolled himself in an alternative high school in Switzerland. He then attended the Federal Institute in Zurich and received his Ph.D. from the University of Zurich in 1905 at age 26.

Upon his graduation from college, Einstein, unable to procure an academic position, took a job as a patent clerk. By day, he worked in the patent office; by night, he worked at home on the groundbreaking theories that would make him famous, such as the photoelectric effect and the Special Theory of Relativity, the theory that led to that most famous of all equations, $E=mc^2$. He published four articles in 1905, the year that has become known as his *annus mirabilis* (miraculous year). A solar eclipse in 1919 proved Einstein's General Theory of Relativity and in 1921, he was awarded the Nobel Prize. Interestingly, he was not awarded the Nobel Prize for the Theory of Relativity, as it was still considered too controversial, but for his work on the photoelectric effect. Einstein, however, recognized where his greatest work lay and delivered his Nobel address on relativity rather than the photoelectric effect.

Einstein's activities were not confined to physics alone. As his career progressed, he wrote and spoke on many global issues including anti-Semitism, racism, and eventually, nuclear disarmament. An ardent pacifist, Einstein was troubled by the fact that his theories contributed to the construction of the most destructive weapon in history, the atomic bomb. Yet, during World War II, he had—contrary to his pacifist beliefs—encouraged the U.S. government in its pursuit of the H-bomb in the face of Hitler's evil. Later, upon viewing the destruction of Hiroshima and Nagasaki, he re-committed himself to pacifism and international cooperation, becoming a supporter of the new United Nations.

The imagination and vision that enabled Einstein to create new theories about how the universe works—from simple visualizations of a man falling from a ladder to those of a person riding a beam of light—also helped him to envision the future, his legacy, and his place in human history. Certain developments in his lifetime, such as the creation of the United Nations, gave him hope, while others, such as the steady proliferation of nuclear arms between the U.S. and USSR during the Cold War, made him worry for the future. Einstein's concerns filled him with a sense of personal responsibility to do what he could to make the world better and safer for all of its inhabitants. It was not enough for Einstein to be a scientist, concerned only with his theories and giving little thought to their practical application. His sense of responsibility for his research and discoveries and for the example he set owing to his celebrity status made him a true humanitarian.

Awareness

Ask students to define *responsibility* in their own words. Discuss the definitions provided at the beginning of this lesson. Ask students to explain how their ideas relate to these definitions of responsibility and to give examples of what responsibility "looks like" in a middle school student, using the above definitions.

Understanding

As they read Stephanie S. MacPherson's *Ordinary Genius* or another biography of Einstein, ask students to recount specific ways that Albert Einstein showed responsibility (keep a record of these examples on a large, prominently displayed chart). Consider his education, his lifework, and his engagement in peace efforts and public and international affairs.

Discuss Einstein's quotation: "I am truly a 'lone traveler' and have never belonged to my country, my home, my friends, or even my immediate family, with my whole heart."

- **What does Einstein mean? How do his actions either confirm or disprove his assertion? Do you believe his claim?**
- **What might such a quote reveal about Einstein's sense of responsibility? What do his actions and words reveal about his attitudes and dispositions and can they be made sense of in light of this quote?**

Action

Activity 1. Recognizing Responsibility

Ask students to each bring in a picture of a person whom they believe consistently displays responsibility. This can be a well-known personality or someone with whom a student regularly interacts. Ask students to write a letter to this person in which they explain 1) the definition of responsibility, and 2) why they chose to write to this person, i.e., several ways in which the person displays this virtue. Students should then ask the person about sources of inspiration (e.g., individuals they admire who exemplify responsibility) in their own lives. Students should actually mail the letter (which may involve tracking down a celebrity's address). The pictures, letters, and responses can be part of a "Responsible Citizens of the World" book or bulletin board display.

Activity 2.
Responsibility
Resolution

Ask students to brainstorm ways that they can practice responsibility in their daily lives. Do they have a pet? Do they baby-sit? Do they have daily/weekly chores to perform? Ask students to make a resolution to be more reliable and/or diligent with regard to a particular responsibility that they struggle with (e.g., their parents are continually reminding them to feed/care for their pet, or they often forget to bring their homework home or to school, etc.). Have students keep a calendar on which they mark off the days/times that they remembered to keep their resolution.

Activity 3.
Responsibility
Reach-Out

Ask students to brainstorm ways in which they can act as "responsible citizens of the world." Ask them to think beyond their own lives to the lives of others—in their school community, in their neighborhoods, in their country, and in the world. Pool the students' ideas and have the class choose one that they will take on as their challenge—either individually or cooperatively. These ideas may include such service projects as canned food drives and beautification projects or such civic-minded projects as letter-writing campaigns.

Reflection

Ask students to reflect on the "Recognizing Responsibility" activity:

- **What motivated the person to whom they chose to write to act responsibly? What have been some of the results of that person's efforts?**
- **Has this person ever failed to act responsibly? What did/would that person do under such circumstances?**
- **What does the habit of being responsible look like?**

Ask students to also reflect on the "Responsibility Resolution" and the "Responsibility Reach-Out."

- **How did the two weeks go? Was the task hard or easy?**
- **What new ideas—large and small—have the students come up with to make the world a better place? What have they learned about the limits and opportunities that individuals have to "make a difference"?**

Invite students to reflect on the kind(s) of contribution(s) they want to make to society. Ask them to write a letter to themselves at the age of 18 that takes their responsibility as citizens and human beings into consideration and that may serve as a reminder of their youthful aspirations as they head off to college. (The students can either seal these letters and save them at home, or the teacher may keep them and mail them to the students upon their graduation from high school.)

- **What type of legacy do they want to leave? What kind of mark do they hope to make on the world?**
- **How far have they come in achieving their dreams?**
- **What type of citizens (of their country, of the world) are they now? What type of citizens would they like to be?**
- **What will they have to do to make a more concerted effort? How do they plan to use their time, talents, and energies in the future?**

Bibliography

Einstein image from:
http://home.pacbell.net/kidwell5/einstein.html

BOOKS
For Students

Goldenstern, J. *Albert Einstein: Physicist and Genius.* Berkley Heights, N.J.: Enslow Publishers, 1995.

MacDonald, R. *Albert Einstein: Genius Behind the Theory of Relativity.* San Diego: Blackbirch Press, 2000.

McPherson, S.S. *Ordinary Genius: The Story of Albert Einstein.* Minneapolis: Carolrhoda Books, 1997.

Severance, J.B. *Einstein: Visionary Scientist.* Boston: Houghton Mifflin, 1999.

For Teachers

Brian, D. *Einstein: A Life.* Hoboken, N.J.: John Wiley & Sons, 1997.

For Students and Teachers

Calaprice, A., Einstein, E., and Schulman, R. *Dear Professor Einstein: Albert Einstein's Letters to and from Children.* Amherst, N.Y.: Prometheus Books, 2002.

FILMS	*Einstein: Light to the Power of 2* (2000; HBO's *Young Inventor Series*)
	Nova: Einstein Revealed (1996)
	A. Einstein: How I See the World (1991)
Also recommended for this lesson:	*Pay It Forward* (2000)
WEB	*Einstein* http://www.amnh.org/exhibitions/einstein
	This feature on the American Museum of Natural History's website provides in-depth information on the life and accomplishments of Albert Einstein.

Character cannot be developed in ease and quiet. Only through experience of trial and suffering can the soul be strengthened, ambition inspired, and success achieved.

—Helen Keller

FORTITUDE

FORTITUDE: The strength of will to patiently endure misfortune for a worthy purpose.

| Deficiency: **Weakness of will** | **FORTITUDE** | Excess: **Stoicism** |

Helen Keller embodied virtues such as courage, perseverance, and hope, but her life stands out as an exemplary model of fortitude. This lesson is intended to introduce students to the virtue of fortitude through Keller's example.

BACKGROUND

The following biographical information serves as a short description of the life of Helen Keller. It is suggested that students read Keller's autobiography, *The Story of My Life,* or another biographical work before beginning this lesson.

Helen Keller was born on June 27, 1880 as a healthy child. The devastating illness that destroyed her senses of sight and hearing overcame Helen when she was 18 months old. Instantly, her life became a tremendous struggle, and Helen found herself unable to communicate with the people around her. She grew frustrated and disobedient. She fought against people who tried to help her, and her parents desperately searched for someone who could communicate with and teach Helen.

The Perkins Institution for the Blind sent a teacher to the Kellers. She was Anne Sullivan, a recent graduate of the Institution and visually impaired herself. Sullivan studied the techniques used to teach fingerspelling to Laura Bridgman, the first deaf and blind child to be educated at the Perkins Institution, and took a train down to the Kellers' home in Tuscumbia, Ala., in March of 1887. Her new pupil was stubborn, strong-willed and used to having her own way, but Sullivan was equally stubborn and strong-willed.

A magical transformation began as soon as Helen's quick young mind made the connection between objects and the strange movements of her teacher's fingers traced out in her palm. Helen began a lifelong, insatiable quest for knowledge. She demanded to know the names of every object around her. She soon mastered Braille, and began to read, expanding her horizons even further. She learned to write, developing a talent that would serve her all her life.[1]

Helen's life unfolded as a story of courage, perseverance, and fortitude. Despite countless obstacles as a result of her physical impairments, she persevered and overcame setbacks. She relates many of these struggles in her autobiography, *The Story of My Life*, which she wrote while in her early twenties.

Helen was once accused of plagiarism, at the age of 11, when her story "The Frost King" closely resembled the work of another author. Helen was devastated because she had no recollection of the other story. Eventually she came to understand that she had confused her own thoughts with a story she had been told. Unintentionally she reproduced these ideas as her own. This conflict discouraged her from writing, but with the encouragement of her teacher, she was able to compose her own thoughts again. Helen was able to recognize the incident as a learning experience; she wrote in her autobiography, "I have given this account of the 'Frost King' affair because it is important in my life and education."[2] Helen displayed humility by share her story and wisdom in realizing that it had been instructive.

At the age of 20, Helen was accepted to Radcliffe College, but not before completing countless hours of entrance examinations. Helen explained that the exams took much longer for her to finish because

> Mr. Keith [one of Helen's former teachers]...had not trained me to write examination papers. Consequently my work was painfully slow, and I had to read the examples over and over before I could form an idea of what I was required to do (p. 57).

Again, Helen chose not to complain:

---

[1]Paragraphs excerpted from http://www.aidb.org/helenkeller/bio.asp
[2]Keller, H. *The Story of My Life*, p. 46.

But I do not blame anyone. The administrative board of Radcliffe did not realize how difficult they were making my examinations, nor did they understand the peculiar difficulties I had to surmount. But if they unintentionally placed obstacles in my way, I have the consolation of knowing that I overcame them all (p. 57).

The desire to learn and achieve kept Helen from giving in to her handicaps. She met challenges with fortitude and found the strength within herself to reach her goals. In her autobiography she describes how she overcame obstacles:

For, after all, every one who wishes to gain true knowledge must climb the Hill Difficulty alone, and since there is no royal road to the summit, I must zigzag it in my own way. I slip back many times, I fall, I stand still, I run against the edge of hidden obstacles, I lose my temper and find it again and keep it better, I trudge on, I gain a little, I feel encouraged, I get more eager and climb higher and begin to see the widening horizon. Every struggle is a victory (p. 59).

As an adult, Keller supported organizations that helped to meet the needs of those who were blind or deaf-blind, such as the Industrial Home for the Blind (which later became known as the Helen Keller Center for the Deaf-Blind Youths and Adults), and the American Association for the Blind. She advocated employment opportunities for the deaf-blind, and she wrote and spoke about blindness and deaf-blindness. She helped to eliminate the practice of institutionalizing the disabled, and she boldly faced the issue of preventing blindness in newborns. Keller received numerous national and international awards for her work, in which she was tirelessly fighting for social reform.

Awareness	Ask students to share what they know about the term *fortitude*. Then provide students with the definition given at the beginning of this lesson and discuss its meaning. Ask for examples of situations in which fortitude is needed.
Understanding	Ask students to share their thoughts on Helen Keller's life and to give examples from her life that illustrate her fortitude.
	Ask students to list ways that they can show fortitude in their daily lives.
	Explain to students that a definition for *stoicism* is "repression of feeling" and "indifference to pleasure and pain." Ask students to discuss the difference between *fortitude* and *stoicism*. Why is one a virtue and the other not? How can we practice fortitude without being stoic?
	Ask students to read the poem *If—* by Rudyard Kipling with a partner. Then ask pairs of students to decide which "If" statements are the best examples of fortitude (patient endurance of misfortune) and which statements best apply to Helen Keller.
Action *"If—"* *by Rudyard Kipling*	Explain to students that Kipling's poem is a guide to living life well. Ask them to write a middle school version of the poem, including "If" statements that are common to their daily lives. These poems should conclude with the statement "then you will be successful in middle school." (Students may write their poems with the intention of sharing them with younger students.) All "If" statements should be positive and should relate to fortitude or courage. Examples include: "If you can ask for a teacher's help without worrying about what other people think of you" and "If you can complete all your homework without giving in to the temptation of television." Display completed poems in the classroom.
Cartoons	Ask students to brainstorm situations that might require fortitude, and to draw cartoons which display fictional characters showing fortitude in those situations. If possible, ask students to agree to use the same characters and compile the stories into an anthology.

Fortitude Challenge	Ask students to seek out ways to show fortitude throughout an entire week. List challenges to overcome and ways to overcome them. Have students write a strategy or action plan. After they have completed the challenge, give them the opportunity to reflect on their experience in an essay or journal entry. Ask volunteers to share their reflections.
Reflection *"Hill Difficulty"*	Keller wrote in her autobiography: "every one who wishes to gain true knowledge must climb the Hill Difficulty" (p.59). Ask students to explain in an essay what is meant by a "Hill Difficulty" or "Difficulty Hill." What are some examples of a Hill Difficulty in middle school? What are the benefits of climbing those specific hills?
On Kipling's "If—"	Pose the question: if Helen Keller were to write her own "If" statements, what might some of them be? What would her ending statement be? (Record students' suggestions on the board.)
On the fortitude challenge	Invite students to reflect on the fortitude challenge. In what situations did they show fortitude? What were the effects? How did they feel as a result?
Bibliography	Keller image from: www2.una.edu/history/ynghelen.jpg
For Students and Teachers	Keller, H. *The Story of My Life*. New York: Airmont, 1965. Helen Keller's autobiography. A challenging read, but excellent for gaining perspective into Helen's life. This publication also includes personal letters to and from Helen Keller, as well as supplementary information on Keller's life and education from others' perspectives. *AIBD Foundation, Helen Keller* http://www.aidb.org/helenkeller/bio.asp *Keller, Helen* http://search.biography.com/print_record.pl?id=16451

If—

Rudyard Kipling

If you can keep your head when all about you
    Are losing theirs and blaming it on you;
If you can trust yourself when all men doubt you,
    But make allowance for their doubting too;
If you can wait and not be tired by waiting,
    Or, being lied about, don't deal in lies,
Or, being hated, don't give way to hating,
    And yet don't look too good, nor talk too wise;

If you can dream—and not make dreams your master;
If you can think—and not make thoughts your aim;
If you can meet with triumph and disaster
    And treat those two impostors just the same;
If you can bear to hear the truth you've spoken
    Twisted by knaves to make a trap for fools,
Or watch the things you gave your life to broken,
    And stoop and build 'em up with worn-out tools;

If you can make one heap of all your winnings
    And risk it on one turn of pitch-and-toss,
And lose, and start again at your beginnings
    And never breathe a word about your loss;
If you can force your heart and nerve and sinew
    To serve your turn long after they are gone,
And so hold on when there is nothing in you
    Except the Will which says to them: "Hold on!"

If you can talk with crowds and keep your virtue,
    Or walk with kings—nor lose the common touch;
If neither foes nor loving friends can hurt you;
    If all men count with you, but none too much;
If you can fill the unforgiving minute
    With sixty seconds' worth of distance run—
Yours is the Earth and everything that's in it,
    And—which is more—you'll be a Man, my son!

A mature person is one who does not think only in absolutes, who is able to be objective even when deeply stirred emotionally, who has learned that there is both good and bad in all people and all things, and who walks humbly and deals charitably with the circumstances of life, knowing that in this world no one is all-knowing and therefore all of us need both love and charity.

—Eleanor Roosevelt

COMPASSION

COMPASSION: The desire to alleviate the sufferings of others.

Deficiency: **Apathy**	—	**COMPASSION**	—	Excess: **Sentimentalism**

Students will study the life of Eleanor Roosevelt during their studies of the Great Depression and of President Franklin D. Roosevelt's New Deal. As "First Lady of the World," her loyalty and service to her husband, her humanitarian efforts during the second World War, her battles against racism, and her fight for the rights of all human beings make her acts of compassion worthy of examination by middle school students.

BACKGROUND

The following biographical information serves as a short description of the life of Eleanor Roosevelt. It is suggested that students read *Eleanor Roosevelt: A Life of Discovery* by Russell Freedman or another biographical work before beginning this lesson.

Eleanor was born into a wealthy family in New York City. She was a shy and awkward young girl whose childhood was marked by sorrow at every turn. She was never close to her mother, who died when Eleanor was very young, but she adored her father, who died of alcoholism two years later. She traveled to England to attend school, where she was encouraged and supported by her teacher, Mademoiselle Souvestre, who recognized her outstanding intellect and her talents as a natural leader.

Roosevelt dreaded making her debut in American society, when a young girl would first attend important social gatherings, but she soon formed a close circle of friends. Among them was Franklin Delano Roosevelt, whom she married in 1905.

Franklin Roosevelt served in the state Senate from 1910 to 1913, which launched Eleanor into the political mainstream. When he was appointed secretary of the Navy and they moved to Washington, she made a strong impression on everyone she met there. In 1921 Franklin was stricken with polio; Eleanor patiently nursed him back to health. She supported Franklin during his campaign for the presidency, and became his eyes and ears, faithfully reporting back to him everything that she learned. When Franklin Delano Roosevelt was elected president, Eleanor completely transformed the function of the First Lady in the White House. Traditionally, the First Lady was expected to host a few formal dinners and remain in her husband's shadow, but Eleanor actively worked for the interests of FDR and for the country. She hosted thousands of guests, held press conferences and gave radio broadcasts, wrote for a newspaper column called "My Day," and traveled all over the world. The First Lady became famous for her boundless energy and graciousness.

Eleanor Roosevelt is most famous for her humanitarian efforts. She served wounded veterans at St. Elizabeth's Hospital during World War I. She was sent to the South Pacific during World War II to boost soldiers' morale. When FDR died in 1945, she said, "The story is over," and retreated to Val-Kill, the cottage that she had built in Hyde Park. Her rest did not last long, however, because soon President Harry S. Truman asked her to serve as a U.S. delegate to the United Nations, and she consented. During her years of service, she helped to draft the *Universal Declaration of Human Rights*, her most famous accomplishment. She resigned from the UN in 1952, but in 1961 President Kennedy reappointed her as the chairperson of the President's Commission on the Status of Women. After so many years of energetic service, Eleanor Roosevelt died in 1962 of tuberculosis. She was mourned around the globe as the "First Lady of the World."

Awareness

Raise students' awarenesss of the virtue of compassion by posting the following quote on the board:

You get more joy out of giving to others and should put a good deal of thought into the happiness you are able to give.

—**Eleanor Roosevelt**

Ask students to define *compassion* and to provide examples of compassionate acts. Compare students' definitions with the definition provided at the beginning of this lesson. Ask students to distinguish compassion from sentimentalism and to use examples to illustrate the difference between the two. Ask them to define *apathy* and discuss what it means to be apathetic toward the needs of others. Have students discuss why people sometimes choose to be apathetic.

Understanding

Provide students with background information on the United Nations and what it means to have a Universal Declaration of Human Rights. Have students find examples of compassion in *Eleanor Roosevelt: A Life of Discovery*. Draw students' attention to Roosevelt's humanitarian efforts as the First Lady and as a delegate to the United Nations, focusing on her work on the United Nations' Universal Declaration of Human Rights.

Action

Classroom declaration of rights

If your school or classroom does not have a fundamental list of rules that foster respect and compassion for others, now might be the appropriate time to write one. Point out the difference between a *right* (such as being free from name-calling) and a *privilege* (such as leaving class without permission). Discuss the connections between rights and responsibilities as well. Ask students to give examples of basic rights to which all human beings should be entitled, and discuss the answers. Then review the Universal Declaration of Human Rights, taking time to translate some of the articles into age-appropriate wording. Determine which of the students' beliefs accord with Eleanor Roosevelt's. Involve the whole class in drafting a document that addresses the rights that students and teachers should have in a school environment. Once the document is completed, help students create a contract with a clear list of rules and consequences designed to "protect their rights," to be signed by all and displayed in the classroom.

Community service project | Follow Eleanor Roosevelt's example of her compassionate efforts throughout the world by reaching out to the local community. Identify and organize a class project such as reading to senior citizens at a nearby nursing home, visiting cancer patients, or cleaning up a local park. Before beginning the project, students should set down specific goals and strategies for reaching these goals. Students should identify the people they think will benefit from this project.

Reflection

On the classroom declaration of rights

A week or two after the signing of the declaration, conduct an in-class discussion about its effectiveness. Continue discussion in monthly updates throughout the school year. How have students been finding the classroom environment since the points in the declaration have been introduced? Are there any rules that need to be added, or that can be improved upon? Have students provide specific examples of any positive changes. Have there been any negative consequences of establishing the declaration of rights? If so, what are they?

On the community service project

Have students write a short essay upon completion of the project. They should answer the following questions:

- **Was the project meaningful?**
- **How did you feel about it? Why?**
- **What did you accomplish?**
- **Were there times during the project when you were reminded of Eleanor Roosevelt? In what ways does she exemplify compassion?**
- **Were there times during the project when you felt frustrated? What did you do in those situations?**
- **What factors made you "stick with" the project?**

On Eleanor Roosevelt: A Life of Discovery

Have students write a one- to two-page page essay answering the following questions:

- **Why do you think that President Truman called Eleanor Roosevelt "First Lady of the World"?**
- **What was the example of compassion in her life that you will remember the most? Why?**
- **What did you learn from her example?**

On the Universal Declaration of Human Rights	Have students write an essay on whether or not having a Universal Declaration of Human Rights is important or even necessary. Are there people who disagree with such rights? How can the UN enforce what most decent people would choose to uphold?
Bibliography	Roosevelt image from: www.wic.org/bio/roosevel.htm
For Students and Teachers	Freedman, R. *Eleanor Roosevelt: A Life of Discovery*. New York: Clarion Books, 1993. Hakim, J. Book Nine: "War, Peace, and All That Jazz." *A History of US*. New York: Oxford University Press, 1999.
For Teachers	*Eleanor Roosevelt* www.udhr.org/history/Biographies/bioer.htm *Franklin D. Roosevelt Library & Digital Archives* www.fdrlibrary.marist.edu *Eleanor Roosevelt: Tribute to Greatness* www.wic.org/bio/roosevel.htm

Where, after all, do universal human rights begin? In small places, close to home—so close and so small that they cannot be seen on any maps of the world. Yet they are the world of the individual person; the neighborhood he lives in; the school or college he attends; the factory, farm, or office where he works. Such are the places where every man, woman, and child seeks equal justice, equal opportunity, equal dignity without discrimination. Unless these rights have meaning there, they have little meaning anywhere. Without concerted citizen action to uphold them close to home, we shall look in vain for progress in the larger world.

—**Eleanor Roosevelt**

Universal Declaration of Human Rights

Adopted and proclaimed by General Assembly resolution 217 A (III)
of 10 December 1948

On December 10, 1948 the General Assembly of the United Nations adopted and proclaimed the Universal Declaration of Human Rights the full text of which appears in the following pages. Following this historic act the Assembly called upon all Member countries to publicize the text of the Declaration and "to cause it to be disseminated, displayed, read and expounded principally in schools and other educational institutions, without distinction based on the political status of countries or territories."

PREAMBLE

Whereas recognition of the inherent dignity and of the equal and inalienable rights of all members of the human family is the foundation of freedom, justice and peace in the world,

Whereas disregard and contempt for human rights have resulted in barbarous acts which have outraged the conscience of mankind, and the advent of a world in which human beings shall enjoy freedom of speech and belief and freedom from fear and want has been proclaimed as the highest aspiration of the common people,

Whereas it is essential, if man is not to be compelled to have recourse, as a last resort, to rebellion against tyranny and oppression, that human rights should be protected by the rule of law,

Whereas it is essential to promote the development of friendly relations between nations,

Whereas the peoples of the United Nations have in the Charter reaffirmed their faith in fundamental human rights, in the dignity and worth of the human person and in the equal rights of men and women and have determined to promote social progress and better standards of life in larger freedom,

Whereas Member States have pledged themselves to achieve, in co-operation with the United Nations, the promotion of universal respect for and observance of human rights and fundamental freedoms,

Whereas a common understanding of these rights and freedoms is of the greatest importance for the full realization of this pledge,

Now, Therefore THE GENERAL ASSEMBLY proclaims THIS UNIVERSAL DECLARATION OF HUMAN RIGHTS as a common standard of achievement for all peoples and all nations, to the end that every individual and every organ of society, keeping this Declaration constantly in mind, shall strive by teaching and education to promote respect for these rights and freedoms and by progressive measures, national and international, to secure their universal and effective recognition and observance, both among the peoples of Member States themselves and among the peoples of territories under their jurisdiction.

Article 1.

All human beings are born free and equal in dignity and rights. They are endowed with reason and conscience and should act towards one another in a spirit of brotherhood.

Article 2.

Everyone is entitled to all the rights and freedoms set forth in this Declaration, without distinction of any kind, such as race, colour, sex, language, religion, political or other opinion, national or social origin, property, birth or other status. Furthermore, no distinction shall be made on the basis of the political, jurisdictional or international status of the country or territory to which a person belongs, whether it be independent, trust, non-self-governing or under any other limitation of sovereignty.

Article 3.

Everyone has the right to life, liberty and security of person.

Article 4.

No one shall be held in slavery or servitude; slavery and the slave trade shall be prohibited in all their forms.

Article 5.

No one shall be subjected to torture or to cruel, inhuman or degrading treatment or punishment.

Article 6.

Everyone has the right to recognition everywhere as a person before the law.

Article 7.

All are equal before the law and are entitled without any discrimination to equal protection of the law. All are entitled to equal protection against any discrimination in violation of this Declaration and against any incitement to such discrimination.

Article 8.

Everyone has the right to an effective remedy by the competent national tribunals for acts violating the fundamental rights granted him by the constitution or by law.

Article 9.

No one shall be subjected to arbitrary arrest, detention or exile.

Article 10.

Everyone is entitled in full equality to a fair and public hearing by an independent and impartial tribunal, in the determination of his rights and obligations and of any criminal charge against him.

Article 11.

(1) Everyone charged with a penal offence has the right to be presumed innocent until proved guilty according to law in a public trial at which he has had all the guarantees necessary for his defence.

(2) No one shall be held guilty of any penal offence on account of any act or omission which did not constitute a penal offence, under national or international law, at the time when it was committed. Nor shall a heavier penalty be imposed than the one that was applicable at the time the penal offence was committed.

Article 12.

No one shall be subjected to arbitrary interference with his privacy, family, home or correspondence, nor to attacks upon his honour and reputation. Everyone has the right to the protection of the law against such interference or attacks.

Article 13.

(1) Everyone has the right to freedom of movement and residence within the borders of each state.

(2) Everyone has the right to leave any country, including his own, and to return to his country.

Article 14.

(1) Everyone has the right to seek and to enjoy in other countries asylum from persecution.

(2) This right may not be invoked in the case of prosecutions genuinely arising from non-political crimes or from acts contrary to the purposes and principles of the United Nations.

Article 15.

(1) Everyone has the right to a nationality.

(2) No one shall be arbitrarily deprived of his nationality nor denied the right to change his nationality.

Article 16.

(1) Men and women of full age, without any limitation due to race, nationality or religion, have the right to marry and to found a family. They are entitled to equal rights as to marriage, during marriage and at its dissolution.

(2) Marriage shall be entered into only with the free and full consent of the intending spouses.

(3) The family is the natural and fundamental group unit of society and is entitled to protection by society and the State.

Article 17.

(1) Everyone has the right to own property alone as well as in association with others.

(2) No one shall be arbitrarily deprived of his property.

Article 18.

Everyone has the right to freedom of thought, conscience and religion; this right includes freedom to change his religion or belief, and freedom, either alone or in community with others and in public or private, to manifest his religion or belief in teaching, practice, worship and observance.

Article 19.

Everyone has the right to freedom of opinion and expression; this right includes freedom to hold opinions without interference and to seek, receive and impart information and ideas through any media and regardless of frontiers.

Article 20.

(1) Everyone has the right to freedom of peaceful assembly and association.

(2) No one may be compelled to belong to an association.

Article 21.

(1) Everyone has the right to take part in the government of his country, directly or through freely chosen representatives.

(2) Everyone has the right of equal access to public service in his country.

(3) The will of the people shall be the basis of the authority of government; this will shall be expressed in periodic and genuine elections which shall be by universal and equal suffrage and shall be held by secret vote or by equivalent free voting procedures.

Article 22.

Everyone, as a member of society, has the right to social security and is entitled to realization, through national effort and international co-operation and in accordance with the organization and resources of each State, of the economic, social and cultural rights indispensable for his dignity and the free development of his personality.

Article 23.

(1) Everyone has the right to work, to free choice of employment, to just and favourable conditions of work and to protection against unemployment.

(2) Everyone, without any discrimination, has the right to equal pay for equal work.

(3) Everyone who works has the right to just and favourable remuneration ensuring for himself and his family an existence worthy of human dignity, and supplemented, if necessary, by other means of social protection.

(4) Everyone has the right to form and to join trade unions for the protection of his interests.

Article 24.

Everyone has the right to rest and leisure, including reasonable limitation of working hours and periodic holidays with pay.

Article 25.

(1) Everyone has the right to a standard of living adequate for the health and well-being of himself and of his family, including food, clothing, housing and medical care and necessary social services, and the right to security in the event of unemployment, sickness, disability, widowhood, old age or other lack of livelihood in circumstances beyond his control.

(2) Motherhood and childhood are entitled to special care and assistance. All children, whether born in or out of wedlock, shall enjoy the same social protection.

Article 26.

(1) Everyone has the right to education. Education shall be free, at least in the elementary and fundamental stages. Elementary education shall be compulsory. Technical and professional education shall be made generally available and higher education shall be equally accessible to all on the basis of merit.

(2) Education shall be directed to the full development of the human personality and to the strengthening of respect for human rights and fundamental freedoms. It shall promote understanding, tolerance and friendship among all nations, racial or religious groups, and shall further the activities of the United Nations for the maintenance of peace.

(3) Parents have a prior right to choose the kind of education that shall be given to their children.

Article 27.

(1) Everyone has the right freely to participate in the cultural life of the community, to enjoy the arts and to share in scientific advancement and its benefits.

(2) Everyone has the right to the protection of the moral and material interests resulting from any scientific, literary or artistic production of which he is the author.

Article 28.

Everyone is entitled to a social and international order in which the rights and freedoms set forth in this Declaration can be fully realized.

Article 29.

(1) Everyone has duties to the community in which alone the free and full development of his personality is possible.

(2) In the exercise of his rights and freedoms, everyone shall be subject only to such limitations as are determined by law solely for the purpose of securing due recognition and respect for the rights and freedoms of others and of meeting the just requirements of morality, public order and the general welfare in a democratic society.

(3) These rights and freedoms may in no case be exercised contrary to the purposes and principles of the United Nations.

Article 30.

Nothing in this Declaration may be interpreted as implying for any State, group or person any right to engage in any activity or to perform any act aimed at the destruction of any of the rights and freedoms set forth herein.

http://www.un.org/Overview/rights.html

I simply can't build up my hopes on a foundation consisting of confusion, misery, and death. I see the world gradually being turned into a wilderness, I hear the ever-approaching thunder, which will destroy us too, I can feel the sufferings of millions and yet, if I look up into the heavens, I think that it will come out all right, that this cruelty too will end, and that peace and tranquility will return again.

—Anne Frank

HOPE

HOPE: The confidence that truth and goodness will prevail, even amid adverse circumstances.

| Deficiency: **Despair** | **HOPE** | Excess: **Naïveté, foolish optimism** |

Students will study the life of Anne Frank as they learn about the Holocaust. During her years in hiding inside the "Secret Annexe," Anne maintained an unwavering faith in the goodness of people, despite her awareness that fellow Jews were being tortured and killed. Her hope and optimism are a good way to show that the human spirit can withstand adverse circumstances.

BACKGROUND

By the time students begin learning about Anne Frank, they should know about the treatment of Jews during the Holocaust. Students will read *Anne Frank: The Diary of a Young Girl* to understand Anne's personal struggles during her two years in hiding. At the teacher's discretion, substitute *Anne Frank: Beyond the Diary* (which has an easier reading level) for Anne's personal diary. This book provides substantial information about the Nazis' treatment of Jews and about the Holocaust, as well as detailed maps, diagrams, and photographs. It also gives an account of what happened to Anne and her family after they were discovered in their Secret Annexe.

Anne Frank was a young Jewish girl who grew up in Holland. Like any other Jewish family who lived in Nazi-occupied Europe, the Franks were subject to Hitler's anti-

Semitic laws. Jews were required to wear a prominent yellow Star of David on their clothing to make them easily identifiable; Jews were forbidden to ride on trains, take a car, or ride a bicycle; Jews had early curfews; Jews could shop only in special Jewish shops, and so forth. Anne's parents made great efforts to protect their children, so Anne never really felt the full impact of these laws until the Nazis began "relocating" the Jews to concentration camps.

On July 5, 1942, Anne's sister Margot received a written summons to report to Westerbork, the transit camp from which she would be sent to a "labor camp." Otto Frank, Anne's father, had been fearing and preparing for the day when one of his family members would be summoned, and he had arranged for his family to go into hiding above the office building where he worked. The Frank family went there in secret the very next day.

Shortly before the Frank family went into hiding, Anne received a diary, which she named "Kitty," for her thirteenth birthday, and she wrote in it frequently over the next two and a half years in the Secret Annexe. Its residents included Anne, her sister Margot, her parents, Mr. and Mrs. Van Pels and their son Peter, and a dentist named Fritz Pfeffer. Everyone had to remain absolutely silent during the daytime because many of the people who worked downstairs did not know that they were hiding, and they were in danger of being discovered and betrayed. They had to be sure not to speak above a quiet whisper; they had to walk softly so that no one could hear footsteps; they could not flush the toilet or cook a meal. But compared to the millions of Jews who were suffering in the concentration or death camps, the Frank family lived relatively comfortably. Anne managed not only to write in her diary, but to keep up with her studies and to write some fictional stories as well.

Life in the annexe was not without its hardships. The living quarters were small and no one was permitted to leave, so confrontations and arguments among residents were common. Acquiring food and the necessary supplies was difficult at times, because the families had to rely entirely on the bravery of friends to smuggle things in. Worst of all was the pervasive fear that they might be found and turned over to the Nazis. The store downstairs was once robbed at night, and the residents always worried that the thief discerned people were hiding upstairs.

Anne Frank's diary is well known not only for its detailed record of the events that took place in the Secret Annexe, but for Anne's examination of her own character and for her insights about her fellow human beings. She felt that she was constantly at war with herself, fighting to obey her better instincts and behave according to her ideals. She never lost hope that the war and cruelty outside the annexe would end, and she steadfastly believed in the goodness of human beings.

After the families had spent two and a half years in hiding, an anonymous caller betrayed the location of the Franks to the Nazis. The Gestapo raided the Secret

Annexe and arrested every one of its residents. When they had been taken away, Miep Gies, one of the brave friends who was helping them survive, managed to go through their belongings and save several documents before the Nazis came back to plunder the rooms. Among these papers was Anne's diary. The prisoners were sent to concentration camps and separated. Surviving prisoners who knew Anne reported that she was always willing to bestow a kind word or a favor upon those who were suffering more than she. Anne Frank died in Bergen-Belsen of starvation and typhus shortly before her sixteenth birthday.

Otto Frank was the only resident of the Secret Annexe to survive the concentration camps. When he returned, Miep Gies presented him with his daughter's diary, which he had published.

Awareness

Despite all the torments that befell the Jews, during the time she was in hiding Anne never failed to hope for a better world. Discuss the following questions with the class:

- **What does *hope* mean? (Then introduce the standard definition to the students.)**
- **Why does hoping require that we face a problem rather than deny that one exists? What is the difference between hope and naïveté?**
- **What is the difference beween hope and delight?**
- **How is wishing for a special gift on your birthday, to use one example, different from the virtue of hope that Anne exhibited?**
- **When and why is hope helpful and good? When and why could it be harmful?**

Understanding

Discuss the following episodes from Anne's diary:

- **The capitulation of Italy (pp. 97-98)**
- **The second St. Nicholas' Day in the Secret Annexe (pp. 108-109)**
- **Anne's appreciation for the good example of their rescuers (pp. 131-132)**

"Our helpers are a very good example...Never have we heard *one* word of the burden which we certainly must be to them, never has one of them complained of all the trouble we give...although others may show heroism in the war or against the Germans, our helpers display heroism in their cheerfulness and affection."

- **Anne's thoughts on happiness (pp. 143, 154)**

"Riches can all be lost, but that happiness in your own heart can only be veiled, and it will still bring you happiness again, as long as you live. As long as you can look fearlessly up into the heavens, as long as you know that you are pure within and that you will still find happiness."

"And whoever is happy will make others happy, too. He who has courage and faith will never perish in misery!"

- **Anne's thoughts on "the good" of going into hiding (pp.153-154)**

"And in the evening, when I lie in bed and end my prayers with the words 'I thank you, God, for all that is good and clear and beautiful,' I am filled with joy. Then I think about 'the good' of going into hiding...I don't think then of all the misery, but of the beauty that still remains."

Then post the following quote:

"In spite of everything, I still believe that people are really good at heart."

Ask students if they find it surprising that Anne Frank wrote this sentence in her diary while she was hiding in the Secret Annexe. How could she believe in the goodness of people when she was aware of all the persecution that was taking place? Why did Anne continue to hope for so long when she could have given up? How would she, or others living with her, have benefited from continuing to hope?

Action

A hope challenge

It is easy for us to become disgruntled about the little things that can go wrong in our everyday lives. Yet some people, like Anne Frank, remain cheerful and optimistic even though they endure tremendous hardship. Anne made a choice to keep her sufferings from affecting her outlook, and we can do the same. Challenge students to make the choice to remain hopeful for a week when life's daily challenges arise, such as:

- poor performance on an assignment
- mistakes in an extracurricular activity
- problems in a relationship with a friend or family member
- physical ailments (sickness, injury)

Students should record instances when they were presented with a challenging situation and yet exhibited the virtue of hope.

Reflection

Meaningful quotes

The fact that Anne's diary has been translated into 55 languages and that over 20 million copies have been sold is testament to its enduring ability to inspire. Have students choose a particularly meaningful passage or quote from the diary and write an essay to explain why it struck them. Ask students to provide examples from their own lives to which the sentiment of the quote could be applied. Perhaps each quote can be posted on a bulletin board in the classroom.

Hope journals

Have students keep "hope journals" in which they record their thoughts about hope. Encourage students to write about their experiences during the period in which they are challenged to be hopeful:

- **What particular challenge did you encounter? How did you react? What did you do?**
- **Were you aware of your attitude towards the difficulty you faced, and did you make an attempt to change it (if it needed changing)? Describe your thoughts and feelings about the experience.**
- **What happened to you as a result, and how did hope change the situation?**

Bibliography

Anne Frank image from http://www.us-israel.org/images/anne1.jpg

For Students and Teachers

Anne Frank: The Diary of a Young Girl. Trans. B.M. Mooyaart. New York: Pocket Books: 1972.

van der Rol, R., and Verhoeven, R. *Anne Frank: Beyond the Diary*. Trans. by Tony Langham and Playm Peters. New York: Penguin Books, 1992.

For Teachers

Müller, Melissa. *Anne Frank*. Trans. Rita and Robert Kimber. New York: Metropolitan Books, 1998.

The Secret Annexe

The Secret Annexe was a building connected to the back of the offices where Bep Voskuijl, Miep Gies, and Johannes Kleiman worked. Otto Frank's old office was on the first floor, as shown here. He and his family hid from the Nazis for two years on the second and third floors, counting on their friends to keep their secret.

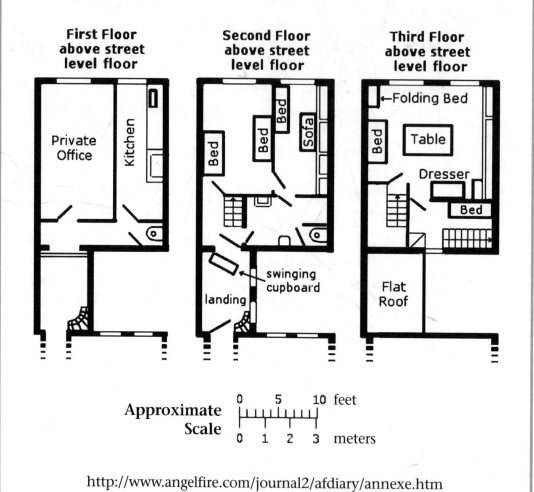

http://www.angelfire.com/journal2/afdiary/annexe.htm

I decided early to give my life to something eternal and absolute. Not to these little gods that are here today and gone tomorrow, but to God who is the same yesterday, today, and forever.

—Martin
Luther King,
*Rediscovering
Lost Values*,
February 28, 1954

INTEGRITY

INTEGRITY: A state of being obtained by standing up for moral principles, regardless of the consequences to oneself; wholeness, being the same person and living up to the same ideals and standards in every situation, public and private.

INTEGRITY*

*Like wisdom, integrity is a virtue that does not fall along a mean. A deficiency of integrity, hypocrisy, can surely exist, but it is the nature of integrity that one can never have too much of it. Integrity is wholeness, and a person can never be too whole.

To deepen their understanding of this critical virtue, students will examine the life of Martin Luther King, Jr. during their studies of the Civil Rights movement. Known worldwide as a man of integrity, Dr. King steadfastly practiced nonviolent resistance to promote the equal rights of blacks and refused to compromise his belief in the cause, even at the expense of his own life.

BACKGROUND

The following biographical information serves as a short description of the life of Martin Luther King, Jr. It is suggested that students read a biography such as *Martin Luther King, Jr.* by John F. Wukovits before beginning this lesson.

Martin Luther King, Jr., a Baptist minister and civil rights leader, was born January 15, 1929, in Atlanta, Ga. He developed talents as a young boy in reading and in orating, which would later become useful in his ministerial work. In 1940, King entered Morehouse College, where he majored in sociology. Upon graduating in 1948, King entered Crozer Theological Seminary to train for the ministry. There he fought to overcome the stereotypes of black men, and his efforts met with great success. One of his teachers said later that King was one of the five best students he had ever taught.

Bob Fitch/Black Star

While he was at Crozer, King attended a lecture on the Indian pacifist Mahatma Gandhi. The lecture provided King the direction he needed for his life. "His message was so profound and electrifying," King later said, "that I left the meeting and bought a half dozen books on Gandhi's life and works." He would later adopt Gandhi's tactics of nonviolent resistance during the Civil Rights movement.

After graduating from Crozer in 1951 with the highest average in his class, King entered Boston University as a doctoral student. There he met his future wife, Coretta Scott, who was studying voice at the New England Conservatory of Music. King received his doctorate from Boston University in 1955 and became pastor of the Dexter Avenue Baptist Church in Montgomery, Ala. The course of his ministry turned to the Civil Rights movement when he joined the supporters of Rosa Parks, a black woman who had been arrested in Montgomery for refusing to give up her bus seat to a white man. King also befriended Ralph Abernathy, a minister with whom he would work for the rest of his life.

In 1957 King and Abernathy were instrumental in founding the Southern Christian Leadership Conference, which became one of several groups King would help to start. On January 14th of that year, King's home and church in Montgomery were bombed as the violence against black protesters continued. After the Montgomery bombing, King said: "Lord, I hope no one will have to die as a result of our struggle for freedom in Montgomery. Certainly I don't want to die. But if anyone has to die, let it be me."

Though always conscious of the possibility of death, King was dedicated to nonviolent resistance because of its power over violence. He adopted Gandhi's idea of *satyagraha*, which combines "truth and love" with "firmness." King knew that hate and violence only beget more hate and violence, but he also knew that black people would have to suffer while adopting a nonviolent stance.

King's life was filled with confrontation, for he was always willing to travel to a scene where he could help demonstrate the power of nonviolence. In March of 1963, the scene was Birmingham, Ala., where blacks were marching and holding demonstrations for equal rights. King joined the marchers and was thrown in jail. During his imprisonment in Birmingham, he wrote a famous letter in the margins of a copy of *The New York Times*. It was in this letter that King gave his rationale for the Civil Rights movement.

On August 28, 1963, King led a march of 250,000 people to Washington, D.C., where both blacks and whites spent a day filled with song and hope and listened to speakers who spoke from the steps of the Lincoln Memorial. As the last speaker of the day, King delivered his "I have a dream" speech in which he stated his hopes for the future. He dreamed of the day when "my four little children...will not be judged by the color of their skin but the content of their character." King ended his talk with the stirring lines: "Free at last! Thank God Almighty, we are free at last!"

King also led a march in Alabama from Selma to Montgomery, which began with 4,000 participants. By the time King reached the state's capital, 25,000 people had joined the march. Rosa Parks marched at the front of the crowd with King.

In 1964 King was awarded the Nobel Peace Prize, becoming its youngest recipient in history. He was always willing to demonstrate peaceably for civil rights in the remaining years of his life, as he did in leading a march across Pettus Bridge in Selma, Ala., on March 21, 1965.

Though a nonviolent person, King was surrounded by enemies who preached violence towards him. He was stabbed in Harlem while autographing copies of his book *Stride Toward Freedom*, but he recovered. King was frequently jailed, which he regarded as a realistic and practical way to symbolize his willingness to suffer for the common good. He expected no less of fellow sympathizers, black and white. Nonviolence "may mean going to jail," he said. "If such is the case the resister must be willing to fill the jail houses of the South. It may even mean physical death. But if physical death is the price a man must pay to free his children and his white brethren from a permanent death of the spirit, then nothing could be more redemptive."

The night before his death, he said, "Like anybody, I would like to live a long time. Longevity has its place. But I'm not concerned about that now. I just want to do God's will. And He's allowed me to go up to the mountain. And I've looked over, and I've seen the Promised Land." He darkened his vision with strong hints of his own doom: "I may not get there with you, but I want you to know tonight that we as a people will get to the Promised Land. So I'm happy tonight. I'm not worried about anything. I'm not fearing any man."

King was assassinated April 4, 1968, on the balcony outside his Memphis motel room. Robert Kennedy quoted Shakespeare's *Romeo and Juliet* when he heard the news:

> When he shall die,
> Take him and cut him out into little stars,
> And he shall make the face of heaven so fine
> That all the world will be in love with night
> And pay no worship to the garish sun.

Awareness

Invite students to list their definitions of integrity, then share the definition at the beginning of this lesson. Ask students to give examples of what integrity "looks like" and "sounds like" in a school setting, at home, at the shopping mall, etc.

Understanding

Ask students to discuss the difference between correcting injustice and "tattling."

Ask students the following questions: Why was Martin Luther King willing to sacrifice his life for what he believed in? Why was fighting for freedom of all Americans more important than his own safety? When someone is willing to stand up for his or her beliefs, no matter what the consequences to himself or herself, we say that that person has *integrity*.

Martin Luther King, Jr., by John F. Wukovits, contains multiple photographs, a timeline of King's life and the Civil Rights movement, an index, and further-reading and works-consulted lists. Have students find examples from this biography that demonstrate King's integrity.

Assign reading of "Letter from a Birmingham City Jail," which King wrote in response to eight white clergymen who had asked African-Americans to be patient for equal rights. Discuss the following questions:

- **What does Martin Luther King mean by "nonviolent resistance" or "civil disobedience"? Give examples of this type of resistance. How could King's portrayal differ from others' use of these methods?**
- **When does King say a law is unjust?**

- **Who are the other men that King labels as "extremists," and how do they support his argument? (The people he lists are Jesus, St. Paul, Amos, Martin Luther, John Bunyan, Abraham Lincoln, and Thomas Jefferson. Students may need more background information on some of these figures.)**
- **Why did some people oppose King? Why would someone want to assassinate him?**

Action
An integrity challenge

Unlike King, we may never need to risk our lives for our beliefs, but we have opportunities to stand up to persecutors every day. For one week, challenge students to practice their integrity when they notice someone being treated unfairly. Brainstorm situations in which students may witness such acts. Identify potential "risks" students might face and discuss what would be entailed in displaying integrity despite those risks. Encourage students to write about their experiences.

Scenes of integrity

Assign students to write short scenes in which a character is faced with a challenging situation and shows integrity in reaching a solution. Students should act out the various scenes. After each role-play, the teacher may direct a discussion of how best to handle the situation. Encourage students to intervene when they see an injustice being committed and, following King's example, do so in a nonviolent, nonaggressive way.

Reflection
On "Letter from a Birmingham City Jail"

Ask students the following questions to begin a class discussion or as an essay prompt.

- **Describe Martin Luther King's notion of "nonviolent resistance," and provide examples of how it can be used effectively in your daily life.**
- **When does King think that we have a moral obligation to disobey the law? Do you agree with him? Why or why not?**

On the integrity challenge

Ask students the following questions to begin a class discussion or as an essay prompt.

- **Did you have an opportunity to stand up to an injustice? What situations presented you with that opportunity?**
- **Describe your thoughts and feelings about the experience.**
- **What factors made it difficult to stand up to injustice?**

An injustice debate | Hold a class debate on the following question.

> · **Do you think that a person who witnesses an injustice and does nothing to stop it can be held accountable for what happens? Why or why not? Use examples to support your answer.**

Bibliography

King image from www.creighton.edu/mlk

For Students and Teachers

Darby, J. *Martin Luther King, Jr.* Minneapolis: Learner Publications Co., 1990.

Hakim, J. Book Ten: *All the People: A History of US.* New York: Oxford University Press, 1999.

January, B. *Martin Luther King, Jr.: Minister and Civil Rights Activist.* Chicago: Ferguson Publishing Co., 2000.

King, M. L. Jr. *I Have a Dream.* New York: Scholastic Trade, 1997.

Martin Luther King Commemorative Collection. Videocassette. MPI Home Video.

Martin Luther King, Jr.: "I Have a Dream." Videocassette. MPI Home Video, 1986.

Wukovits, J. F. *Martin Luther King, Jr.* San Diego: Lucent Books, 1999.

For Teachers

Martin Luther King's *Letter from Birmingham Jail*
http://www.almaz.com/nobel/peace/MLK-jail.html

King, Martin Luther, Jr.
http://search.biography.com/print_record.pl?id=16554

Martin Luther King Jr., A LIFE Tribute
http://www.lifemag.com/Life/mlk/

The Martin Luther King Jr. Papers Project
http://www.stanford.edu/group/King

Martin Luther King:
"Letter from a Birmingham City Jail" (1963)

AUTHOR'S NOTE: This response to a published statement by eight fellow clergymen from Alabama (Bishop C. C. J. Carpenter, Bishop Joseph A. Durick, Rabbi Hilton L. Grafman, Bishop Paul Hardin, Bishop Holan B. Harmon, the Reverend George M. Murray. the Reverend Edward V. Ramage and the Reverend Earl Stallings) was composed under somewhat constricting circumstance. Begun on the margins of the newspaper in which the statement appeared while I was in jail, the letter was continued on scraps of writing paper supplied by a friendly Negro trusty, and concluded on a pad my attorneys were eventually permitted to leave me. Although the text remains in substance unaltered, I have indulged in the author's prerogative of polishing it for publication.

April 16, 1963

MY DEAR FELLOW CLERGYMEN:

While confined here in the Birmingham city jail, I came across your recent statement calling my present activities "unwise and untimely." Seldom do I pause to answer criticism of my work and ideas. If I sought to answer all the criticisms that cross my desk, my secretaries would have little time for anything other than such correspondence in the course of the day, and I would have no time for constructive work. But since I feel that you are men of genuine good will and that your criticisms are sincerely set forth, I want to try to answer your statements in what I hope will be patient and reasonable terms.

I think I should indicate why I am here in Birmingham, since you have been influenced by the view which argues against "outsiders coming in." I have the honor of serving as president of the Southern Christian Leadership Conference, an organization operating in every southern state, with headquarters in Atlanta, Georgia. We have some eighty-five affiliated organizations across the South, and one of them is the Alabama Christian Movement for Human Rights. Frequently we share staff, educational and financial resources with our affiliates. Several months ago the affiliate here in Birmingham asked us to be on call to engage in a nonviolent direct-action program if such were deemed necessary. We readily consented, and when the hour came we lived up to our promise. So I, along with several members of my staff, am here because I was invited here I am here because I have organizational ties here.

But more basically, I am in Birmingham because injustice is here. Just as the prophets of the eighth century B.C. left their villages and carried their "thus saith the Lord" far beyond the boundaries of their home towns, and just as the Apostle Paul left his village of Tarsus and carried the gospel of Jesus Christ to the far corners of the Greco-Roman world, so am I. compelled to carry the gospel of freedom beyond my own home town. Like Paul, I must constantly respond to the Macedonian call for aid.

Moreover, I am cognizant of the interrelatedness of all communities and states. I cannot sit idly by in Atlanta and not be concerned about what happens in Birmingham. Injustice anywhere is a threat to justice everywhere. We are caught in an inescapable network of mutuality, tied in a single garment of destiny. Whatever affects one directly, affects all indirectly. Never again can we afford to live with the narrow, provincial "outside agitator" idea. Anyone who lives inside the United States can never be considered an outsider anywhere within its bounds.

You deplore the demonstrations taking place in Birmingham. But your statement, I am sorry to say, fails to express a similar concern for the conditions that brought about the demonstrations. I am sure that none of you would want to rest content with the superficial kind of social analysis that deals merely with effects and does not grapple with underlying causes. It is unfortunate that demonstrations are taking place in Birmingham, but it is even more unfortunate that the city's white power structure left the Negro community with no alternative....

You may well ask: "Why direct action? Why sit-ins, marches and so forth? Isn't negotiation a better path?" You are quite right in calling for negotiation. Indeed, this is the very purpose of direct action. Nonviolent direct action seeks to create such a crisis and foster such a tension that a community which has constantly refused to negotiate is forced to confront the issue. It seeks so to dramatize the issue that it can no longer be ignored. My citing the creation of tension as part of the work of the nonviolent-resister may sound rather shocking. But I must confess that I am not afraid of the word "tension." I have earnestly opposed violent tension, but there is a type of constructive, nonviolent tension which is necessary for growth.

Just as Socrates felt that it was necessary to create a tension in the mind so that individuals could rise from the bondage of myths and half-truths to the unfettered realm of creative analysis and objective appraisal, we must see the need for nonviolent gadflies to create the kind of tension in society that will help men rise from the dark depths of prejudice and racism to the majestic heights of understanding and brotherhood.

The purpose of our direct-action program is to create a situation so crisis-packed that it will inevitably open the door to negotiation. I therefore concur with you in your call for negotiation. Too long has our beloved Southland been bogged down in a tragic effort to live in monologue rather than dialogue...

We know through painful experience that freedom is never voluntarily given by the oppressor; it must be demanded by the oppressed. Frankly, I have yet to engage in a direct-action campaign that was "well timed" in the view of those who have not suffered unduly from the disease of segregation. For years now I have heard the word "Wait!" It rings in the ear of every Negro with piercing familiarity. This "Wait" has almost always meant "Never." We must come to see, with one of our distinguished jurists, that "justice too long delayed is justice denied."

We have waited for more than 340 years for our constitutional and God-given rights. The nations of Asia and Africa are moving with jetlike speed toward gaining political independence, but we still creep at horse-and-buggy pace toward gaining a cup of coffee at a lunch counter. Perhaps it is easy for those who have never felt the stinging dark of segregation to say, "Wait." But when you have seen vicious mobs lynch your mothers and fathers at will and drown your sisters and brothers at whim; when you have seen hate-filled policemen curse, kick and even kill your black brothers and sisters; when you see the vast majority of your twenty million Negro brothers smothering in an airtight cage of poverty in the midst of an affluent society; when you suddenly find your tongue twisted and your speech stammering as you seek to explain to your six-year-old daughter why she can't go to the public amusement park that has just been advertised on television, and see tears welling up in her eyes when she is told that Funtown is closed to colored children, and see ominous clouds of inferiority beginning to form in her little mental sky, and see her beginning to distort her personality by developing an unconscious bitterness toward white people; when you have to concoct an answer for a five-year-old son who is asking: "Daddy, why do white people treat colored people so mean?"; when you take a cross-county drive and find it necessary to sleep night after night in the uncomfortable corners of your automobile because no motel will accept you; when you are humiliated day in and day out by nagging signs reading "white" and "colored"; when your first name becomes "nigger," your middle name becomes "boy" (however old you are) and your last name becomes "John," and your wife and mother are never given the respected title "Mrs."; when you are harried by day and haunted by night by the fact that you are a Negro, living constantly at tiptoe stance, never quite knowing what to expect next, and are plagued with inner fears and outer resentments; when you know forever fighting a degenerating sense of "nobodiness" then you will understand why we find it difficult to wait. There comes a time when the cup of endurance runs over, and men are no longer willing to be plunged into the abyss of despair. I hope, sirs, you can understand our legitimate and unavoidable impatience.

You express a great deal of anxiety over our willingness to break laws. This is certainly a legitimate concern. Since we so diligently urge people to obey the Supreme Court's decision of 1954 outlawing segregation in the public schools, at first glance it may seem rather paradoxical for us consciously to break laws. One may now ask: "How can you advocate breaking some laws and obeying others?" The answer lies in the fact that there are two types of laws: just and unjust. I would be the Brat to advocate obeying just laws. One has not only a legal but a moral responsibility to obey just laws. Conversely, one has a moral responsibility to disobey unjust laws. I would agree with St. Augustine that "an unjust law is no law at all."

Now, what is the difference between the two? How does one determine whether a law is just or unjust? A just law is a man-made code that squares with the moral law or the law of God. An unjust law is a code that is out of harmony with the moral law. To put it in the terms of St. Thomas Aquinas: An unjust law is a human law that is not rooted in eternal law and natural law. Any law that uplifts human personality is just. Any law that degrades human personality is unjust. All segregation statutes are unjust because segregation distorts the soul and damages the personality. It gives the segregator a false sense of superiority and the segregated a false sense of inferiority. Segregation, to use the terminology of the Jewish philosopher Martin Buber, substitutes an "I-it" relationship for an "I-thou" relationship and ends up relegating persons to the status of things. Hence segregation is not only politically, economically and sociologically unsound, it is morally wrong and awful. Paul Tillich said that sin is separation. Is not segregation an existential expression of man's tragic separation, his awful estrangement, his terrible sinfulness? Thus it is that I can urge men to obey the 1954 decision of the Supreme Court, for it is morally right; and I can urge them to disobey segregation ordinances, for they are morally wrong.

Let us consider a more concrete example of just and unjust laws. An unjust law is a code that a numerical or power majority group compels a minority group to obey but does not make binding on itself. This is difference made legal. By the same token, a just law is a code that a majority compels a minority to follow and that it is willing to follow itself. This is sameness made legal.

Let me give another explanation. A law is unjust if it is inflicted on a minority that, as a result of being denied the right to vote, had no part in enacting or devising the law. Who can say that the legislature of Alabama which set up that state's segregation laws was democratically elected? Throughout Alabama all sorts of devious methods are used to prevent Negroes from becoming registered voters, and there are some counties in which, even though Negroes constitute a majority of the population, not a single Negro is registered. Can any law enacted under such circumstances be considered democratically structured?

Sometimes a law is just on its face and unjust in its application. For instance, I have been arrested on a charge of parading without a permit. Now, there is nothing wrong in having an ordinance which requires a permit for a parade. But such an ordinance becomes unjust when it is used to maintain segregation and to deny citizens the First Amendment privilege of peaceful assembly and protest.

I hope you are able to see the distinction I am trying to point out. In no sense do I advocate evading or defying the law, as would the rabid segregationist. That would lead to anarchy. One who breaks an unjust law must do so openly, lovingly, and with a willingness to accept the penalty. I submit that an individual who breaks a law that conscience tells him is unjust and who willingly accepts the penalty of imprisonment in order to arouse the conscience of the community over its injustice, is in reality expressing the highest respect for law.

Of course, there is nothing new about this kind of civil disobedience. It was evidenced sublimely in the refusal of Shadrach, Meshach and Abednego to obey the laws of Nebuchadnezzar, on the ground that a higher moral law was at stake. It was practiced superbly by the early Christians, who were willing to face hungry lions and the excruciating pain of chopping blocks rather than submit to certain unjust laws of the Roman Empire. To a degree, academic freedom is a reality today because Socrates practiced civil disobedience. In our own nation, the Boston Tea Party represented a massive act of civil disobedience.

We should never forget that everything Adolf Hitler did in Germany was "legal" and everything the Hungarian freedom fighters did in Hungary was "illegal." It was "illegal" to aid and comfort a Jew in Hitler's Germany. Even so, I am sure that, had I lived in Germany at the time, I would have aided and comforted my Jewish brothers. If today I lived in a Communist country where certain principles dear to the Christian faith are suppressed, I would openly advocate disobeying that country's antireligious laws...

Oppressed people cannot remain oppressed forever. The yearning for freedom eventually manifests itself, and that is what has happened to the American Negro. Something within has reminded him of his birthright of freedom, and something without has reminded him that it can be gained. Consciously or unconsciously, he has been caught up by the Zeitgeist, and with his black brothers of Africa and his brown and yellow brothers of Asia, South America and the Caribbean, the United States Negro is moving with a sense of great urgency toward the promised land of racial justice. If one recognizes this vital urge that has engulfed the Negro community, one should readily understand why public demonstrations are taking place. The Negro has many pent-up resentments and latent frustrations, and he must release them. So let him march; let him make prayer pilgrimages to the city hall; let him go on freedom rides—and try to understand why he must do so. If his repressed emotions are not released in nonviolent ways, they will seek expression through violence; this is not a threat but a fact of history. So I have not said to my people: "Get rid of your discontent." Rather, I have tried to say that this normal and healthy discontent can be channeled into the creative outlet of nonviolent direct action. And now this approach is being termed extremist.

But though I was initially disappointed at being categorized as an extremist, as I continued to think about the matter I gradually gained a measure of satisfaction from the label. Was not Jesus an extremist for love: "Love your enemies, bless them that curse you, do good to them that hate you, and pray for them which despitefully use you, and persecute you." Was not Amos an extremist for justice: "Let justice roll down like waters and righteousness like an ever-flowing stream." Was not Paul an extremist for the Christian gospel: "I bear in my body the marks of the Lord Jesus." Was not Martin Luther an extremist: "Here I stand; I cannot do otherwise, so help me God." And John Bunyan: "I will stay in jail to the end of my days before I make a butchery of my conscience." And Abraham Lincoln: "This nation cannot survive half slave and half free." And Thomas Jefferson: "We hold these truths to be self-evident, that all men are created equal..." So the question is not whether we will be extremists, but what kind of extremists we will be. Will we be extremists for hate or for love? Will we be extremist for the preservation of injustice or for the extension of justice? In that dramatic scene on Calvary's hill three men were crucified. We must never forget that all three were crucified for the same crime—the crime of extremism. Two were extremists for immorality, and thus fell below their environment. The other, Jesus Christ, was an extremist for love, truth and goodness, and thereby rose above his environment. Perhaps the South, the nation and the world are in dire need of creative extremists...

I hope the church as a whole will meet the challenge of this decisive hour. But even if the church does not come to the aid of justice, I have no despair about the future. I have no fear about the outcome of our struggle in Birmingham, even if our motives are at present misunderstood. We will reach the goal of freedom in Birmingham, and all over the nation, because the goal of America is freedom. Abused and scorned though we may be, our destiny is tied up with America's destiny. Before the pilgrims landed at Plymouth, we were here. Before the pen of Jefferson etched the majestic words of the Declaration of Independence across the pages of history, we were here. For more than two centuries our forebears labored in this country without wages; they made cotton king; they built the homes of their masters while suffering gross injustice and shameful humiliation—and yet out of a bottomless vitality they continued to thrive and develop. If the inexpressible cruelties of slavery could not stop us, the opposition we now face will surely fail. We will win our freedom because the sacred heritage of our nation and the eternal will of God are embodied in our echoing demands...

I hope this letter finds you strong in the faith. I also hope that circumstances will soon make it possible for me to meet each of you, not as an integrationist or a civil rights leader but as a fellow clergyman and a Christian brother. Let us all hope that the dark clouds of racial prejudice will soon pass away and the deep fog of misunderstanding will be lifted from our fear-drenched communities, and in some not too distant tomorrow the radiant stars of love and brotherhood will shine over our great nation with all their scintillating beauty.

Yours for the cause
of Peace and Brotherhood,

MARTIN LUTHER KING, JR.

Reprinted by arrangement with the Estate of Martin Luther King Jr., c/o Writers House as agent for the proprietor New York, NY.

Copyright 1963 Martin Luther King Jr., copyright renewed 1991 Coretta Scott King

GREAT LIVES LESSON PLAN EVALUATION

Center for the Advancement of Ethics and Character Lesson Review Form

Name: _____

School/District:_____

Address: _____

Street: _____ City: _____

State or Province and zip code: _____

Country: _____

E-Mail:_____

Which *Great Lives* lesson did you use?_____

At which grade level was this lesson used?

☐ 5th grade   ☐ 6th grade   ☐ 7th grade   ☐ 8th grade

Other_____

In which subject area(s) was the lesson used?

☐ All/General   ☐ Languages/Language Arts   ☐ History/Social Studies

☐ Science   ☐ Art/Music   ☐ Math

Other_____

Which lesson activities did you use? (Please describe briefly.)

Awareness _____

_____

_____

_____

Understanding _____

_____

_____

_____

Action _____

_____

_____

_____

Reflection _____

_____

_____

_____

In what ways did you modify the lesson to make it more appropriate for your students or subject area?

_____

_____

_____

What (if any) extra materials or resources did you use?

_____

_____

_____

Use a scale of 1 to 5 to rate the items below. 1=poor, 5=excellent

Use of _____'s life to exemplify virtue.

        1   2   3   4   5

Clarity of the lesson and usefulness as part of your curriculum.

        1   2   3   4   5

Awareness of the life of the individual and his/her virtuous quality prompted by the lesson

        1   2   3   4   5

Understanding of the value of the virtue generated by the lesson

        1   2   3   4   5

Increased internalization of the virtue encouraged by the lesson

        1   2   3   4   5

The extent to which the lesson prompted student reflection on the value of a virtue within their own life and that of the highlighted individual

        1   2   3   4   5

Additional comments: _____

_____

_____

Please return form to: The Center for the Advancement of Ethics and Character (CAEC), Boston University, 621 Commonwealth Avenue, 4th floor, Boston, MA 02215; or fax to: (617) 353-4351.

CURRICULUM DEVELOPMENT

Using the Internalizing Virtue Framework with Great Lives

This worksheet may be usefully completed both by individual teachers and by teachers working collaboratively within subject areas or in interdisciplinary groups. Answer the following questions for each of the four teaching goals that help students move from awareness to an internalization of virtue.

Identify a Great Life

Name an individual from history or present-day life who can be studied to help students understand how virtue contributes to choosing wisely.

_____

1. Building Awareness

- What virtues (habits of mind, heart, and action) are illustrated through the life of this person?
- How will you define the virtue(s) for your students?

2. Inspiring Understanding

- What biographies, narratives, films, works of art, primary-source documents, or other curricular materials might be used to provide students with both rich background about this individual's life and insight into the choices she/he made?
- How could you use this content to move and inspire students?
- How could you use examples and images from these sources to help students identify and examine the difference between wise and poor choices?

3. Developing Habits of Action (helping students practice virtue and choose well)

- What activities, behavioral expectations, or projects would invite students to practice the virtue revealed through the Great Life more consistently?
- How could you create opportunities for students to practice making and acting on good choices?
- How will you invite students to set practical goals for making good choices in school?

4. Fostering Reflection (helping students analyze, judge, critique, and make distinctions)

- In studying this individual's life and contributions, what thought-provoking questions can be framed to prompt writing and discussion?

- How can you help students to recognize the difference between a virtuous choice and choice based on convenience or self-satisfaction?

- What questions emerge from the study of this Great Life that could help students explore the ethical dimensions and impact of individual choices?

- What questions/activities could engage students in a deeper exploration of the virtue(s) exemplified by this individual? (Consider the Aristotelian scale.)

- What opportunities can you create to challenge students to recognize why this virtue(s) is important to their own lives?

The goal of this exercise is *not* to promote inappropriate self-disclosure, but to identify those habits of mind, heart, and action that will enable students to choose wisely in the classroom, on the sports field, in the hallways, on the school bus, and in the cafeteria.